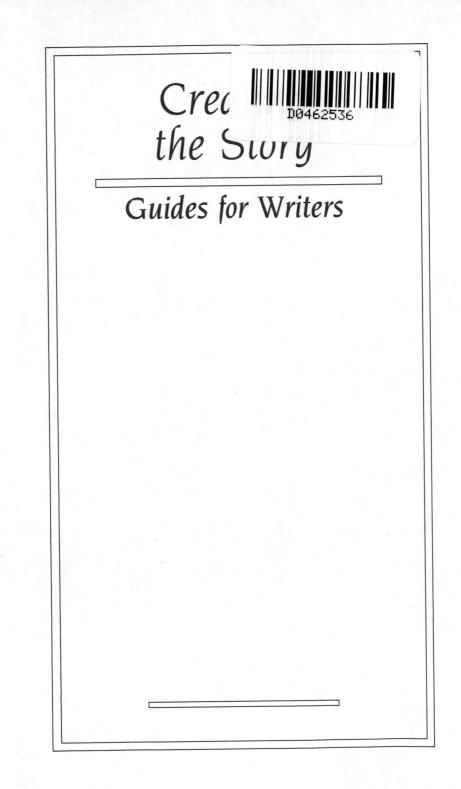

Crea the Story

Guides for Writers

Creating
the Story

Guides for Writers

Rebecca Rule & Susan Wheeler

HEINEMANN
PORTSMOUTH, NEW HAMPSHIRE

Heinemann
A division of Reed Elsevier Inc.
361 Hanover Street, Portsmouth, NH 03801-3912
Offices and agents throughout the world.

Every effort has been made to contact the copyright holders for
permission to reprint borrowed material. We regret any oversights that
may have occurred and would be happy to rectify them in future
printings of this work.

Library of Congress Cataloging-in-Publication Data
Rule, Rebecca.
    Creating the story : guides for writers / Rebecca Rule and
Susan Wheeler.
        p.   cm.
    Includes bibliographical references and index.
    ISBN 0-435-08765-7
    1. Fiction—Authorship.   2. Creative writing.   I. Wheeler, Susan,
    1936–   II. Title.
    PN3355.R85   1993
    808.3–dc20   92-30964
                                                                  CIP

Back-cover photo of Rebecca Rule by Ron St. Jean.
Designed by Joni Doherty.
Printed in the United States of America.
04 03 02 01   DA   8 9 10 11 12

To Jean & Bud Barker

And to Walker, Shel, & Margot Wheeler

Contents

CONTENTS

Acknowledgments

Dawn Boyer asked us for a book about writing and helped us on this one. She's a wonderful editor, collaborator, and friend. We also thank Charles Boyer, the copyeditor, for his careful work. Both of them helped us enormously.

We thank our readers who offered excellent suggestions including Jim Connor, Margaret-Love Denman, Ursula Hegi, Alice McDermott, and Elizabeth Whaley.

We thank our students for telling us what worked and what didn't in our drafts. Thanks especially to the students in the University of New Hampshire Summer Studies 1991, in the fiction writing courses at U.N.H. and U.N.H. Manchester 1991, and in the EXCEL Creative Writing Class at Noble High School in Berwick, Maine.

We confess to having stolen ideas from so many teachers at U.N.H. that we've lost track of who should get credit for what, but we know we owe special thanks to Bruce Ballenger, Margaret-Love Denman, Don Graves, Jean Kennard, Barry Lane, Andy Merton, Don Murray, Tom Newkirk, Gail Pass, Janet Schofield, Mark Smith, Virginia Stuart, Ted Weesner, the late Thomas Williams, and John Yount.

Thanks also to John Rule, Adi Rule, Sarah Smith, Joann Bailey, Carolyn Page, Roy Zarucchi, Marion Ellis, Emily Smith, E.B.B., and the Friday group for unwavering encouragement on many levels.

Letter to a new writer

WE WROTE CREATING THE STORY: GUIDES FOR WRITERS TO help you write stories. We believe that you have wonderful people and worlds to write about and that if you study the craft and write and revise many times, you will bring these people and worlds to life in stories. It takes time. If you wanted to be an opera singer or a painter or a skater, you'd expect to spend years practicing. Worthwhile disciplines require long apprenticeships.

Our guides are practical and short. You can read them in any order, dipping in and out according to your interest and need. We include discussions about the writing process and about attitudes toward craft such as writing often, honestly, and confidently. We demonstrate the skills all fiction writers rely on to tell their tales, such as using details; writing scenes, beginnings, and endings; and summarizing and stretching time.

We repeat information and advice occasionally because all elements of fiction connect and interweave; however, we emphasize slightly different angles of vision each time.

We urge you to avoid pre-plotted, gimmicky stories. You'll become much more deeply involved in and fascinated by your stories if you write for depth—that is, if you write to discover insights into your main characters rather than stuffing them in corsets and shoving them about into preconceived plots. We also urge you to develop the writer's eye for essential, outstanding details, and we stress finding the right words.

We illustrate many points by referring to published fiction, including our own. We've chosen certain stories because we love and respect them for many reasons; we've chosen them because they illustrate specific strengths, skills, and techniques that we feel all writers should know about. For instance, Toni Cade Bambara's narrator in "The Hammer Man," has a vibrant, unforgettable voice. Bambara's stories are often about African-Americans, and in this story as in many of her others, the language is earthy, pithy, immediate. James Joyce can teach us, among a thousand other things, how to have our characters think on the page. Gabriel García Márquez mixes fantasy and reality. Flannery O'Connor has an extraordinary eye for detail and she can show us how to get into characters' minds.

Throughout the book, we stress the importance of reading like a writer. We will help you to bring a magnifying glass to the page so you can study the writing craft and steal techniques that you can apply to your work. At the end of this book we list where you can find these stories, and we recommend a number of anthologies and collections we feel you should know.

Most guides end with writing exercises. Many of these exercises are original, designed to give you practice with specific skills and ideas for short stories of your own. For instance, following the guide that shows you how to write dramatic scenes, we suggest you think of an argument you had with someone you feel strongly about—or you can think about a fictional character who has an argument with someone. Then you write that argument as a dramatic scene. We've found that from this exercise, stories often emerge—after all, the heart of a story lies in conflict, and this exercise is bred of it. In fact, we can't imagine anyone *not* getting ideas for stories from most of these exercises.

We trust you'll ignore any guide if it gets in the way of the truth of your story.

The book grew from our experiences as fiction writers and teachers. Both of us have published short stories and have taught undergraduates in fiction workshops at the University of New Hampshire. Rebecca Rule also teaches graduate students at U.N.H.—people who teach from college to kinder-garten and who want to study fiction so they can teach it better. Susan Wheeler teaches fiction classes for a week each summer at the Molasses Pond Writers Conference in Maine for writers of all ages. Both of us have been visiting teachers in public high schools. The needs of the different students we have taught are remarkably the same, because the demands of short story writing remain the same; for years we've looked for a textbook that could meet these needs, a textbook with brief, accessible explanations of writing skills, and with quick discussions on good attitudes about writing fiction—the kind of nuts-and-bolts advice that we have received from our writing friends and teachers and have passed along in classes and conferences to our students. We've wanted a book that encourages new writers, and explains, in a little more depth than we have time for in one semester, some of the major points we make in class.

We see our book as a Strunk and White *Elements of Style* for fiction writers: short, practical, no nonsense. We believe that like *Elements of Style*, our book will be useful for writers of all ages in colleges and high schools, and by writers writing without teachers.

As we wrote, we tried out guides with our classes who would tell us: "Yes, this was really helpful"; or "No, you missed there"; or "Give us more examples." Now as we send this out to you, we feel ourselves pulling at your sleeve from time to time to say as we do to our students: Come on, start writing, and remember that everyone loves a good story.

GETTING STARTED

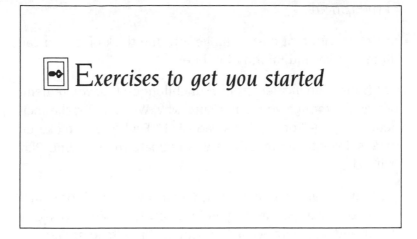

Exercises to get you started

BEFORE YOU READ FURTHER, YOU MAY WANT TO START writing, get some ideas down, get a story or two going. Try one or more of these quick-start exercises that we discuss in greater detail further on in the book. See what happens.

1. Think of a flaw that has gotten you in trouble, such as drinking too much, spending too much money, gossiping, procrastinating, being too aggressive or passive or gloomy or manic, losing your temper, lying, cheating, being a slob, being compulsively neat, being unfaithful to a friend or lover. Give this flaw to a character—about your age or younger—and place her in a world that's familiar to you, for instance, in a family, school, job, or activity you know well. Name your character and invent how she looks, dresses, behaves. Know what hangs on her walls, what music she plays, what movies she likes. Then exaggerate the flaw. Next, place your character in a *specific* conflict that was brought on as a result of the flaw. If, for instance, your character has been unfaithful, her lover may have discovered what has been going on and, as the story opens, is confronting her. Start with the specific conflict precipitated by the flaw.

2. Think of someone who gets you riled, someone you can't stand, or perhaps better, someone you both love and hate at the same time. Exaggerate the "sins" of this other person, magnify the problem you have with him. Think of or invent a specific incident where the long-term problem comes to crisis

and start with that crisis. Plunge into the thick of it. You can fill in background information later.

3. Think of an incident from your childhood that you remember vividly though you're not sure why. Write about the incident using "he" or "she" instead of "I." Feel free to make up details, invent, and modify as you recreate the incident. Play "what if."

4. Think of an experience where you saw yourself or someone critically important to you in a new way. Write to see in detail and in depth what happened. Write to discover the meaning of the experience.

5. Think of a time when you behaved poorly, disappointed yourself. Invent a character who behaved even worse than you did. Make this character less able to cope than you, more vulnerable, slightly less intelligent than you, and have compassion for his bumblings. Write about what happened to him.

6. Start a story with an object you feel strongly about, such as a hearing aid, an old car that breaks down often, a disagreeable roommate's stinking socks, an ugly vase given to you for Christmas. You should feel conflicted about the object and/or about something or someone associated with it. Describe the object in detail. You will gradually discover the character behind the description. Set the character in contact with the object. See what happens.

7. Think of a relationship with someone or with an institution that has caused you distress, conflict. Play "what if," exaggerate the trouble and write about it.

8. In the middle of a page write an evocative word like "jealousy," "grief," "grudge," "marriage," "grades," "failure," "blood," "storm," "hate," "fear," "loss," "police." The word must hold strong meaning for you, and since stories are about trouble and conflict, the word should reverberate negatively. Web your associations with the word, drawing lines from

the center word to one association you make, then another and another. Be susceptible to conflicts, characters, story possibilities.

9. List your territories: places, activities, jobs, and worlds you know well. Examples: deep-sea fishing, being a friend, an enemy, a student, a brother or the eldest daughter, getting in trouble with the police or at school or at work, baking pies, going to rock concerts, procrastinating, hanging out with friends, collecting wild flowers, repairing motorcycles. These are areas of authority, useful in determining where to set your stories, what your characters do, what they think about, what they know. Now list people and events that caused or now cause you conflict and that are associated with these territories.

Have confidence

OF COURSE YOU CAN WRITE STORIES. YOU'VE BEEN TELLING and hearing them since you could talk. You've probably read a number of them, too.

Think of the best stories you've heard. The tellers cared deeply, needed to tell about what happened, knew that what they had to say was interesting, and knew you would care.

When you write, you need that kind of confidence. You must believe that this character and what happens to him will fascinate readers because it fascinates you. You must believe that with work you can create a story with life, shape, and meaning. You must believe that you have a wonderful story to tell.

Storytellers and story writers who let anxieties and lack of confidence get in the way will falter. They will be *self*-conscious rather than *story*-conscious.

What can we say to help you gain confidence? Well, first, let's get rid of this notion that there are WRITERS and pitiful beginners. Yes, there are published writers whose work you'll love, admire, and learn from. But don't discourage yourself with comparison. Instead, recognize that you are a new writer who has joined a community of writers. We like to think there's a perfect short story out there to be written. Of course it never will be, but we're all trying for it. Your favorite published writers are further along than you, and, as you study their fiction, you'll pick up ideas and craft from them.

Many new writers undermine their confidence with awful doubts: "This is boring. Who cares! I haven't got the talent and brains." Published writers have these doubts, too; but somehow we put doubts aside as we write, becoming more concerned with our stories than our insecurities. You must learn to do this, too.

We would like to order you to have confidence, to say to you, "Have confidence, dammit!" But it's up to you. You must make a decision to believe in your ability to write a story, believe in your characters and their problems, believe in the potential of your story as you write. Yes, writing's hard work. Katherine Anne Porter said she rewrote her first published story, "Flowering Judas," fifteen or sixteen times. Hemingway rewrote the ending of A *Farewell to Arms* thirty-nine times. You'll revise endlessly and will suffer periods of terrible discouragement as all writers do, but you will write stories. Of course you will.

What is a story?

THERE'S A MYSTERY TO WHAT MAKES A STORY GREAT THAT can never be entirely understood, but stories do have common elements we can talk about. A story is about people. About people in trouble, or conflict. Something happens. Often a new light is shed on someone or something. A story starts with conflict or tension that keeps mounting until it erupts near the end in a crisis, or until an epiphany is reached. Or there can be several eruptions throughout the story. But at the end, when that crisis point explodes or that moment of revelation is achieved, there is a turning point, a falling off of the action, and resolution. Life thereafter is never exactly the same. Your main character's life may be radically changed. More often, she will have a new way of seeing or feeling or thinking about someone or something. Immediately we think of an exception—there are always exceptions: the story where your main character has a chance to change, to see something in a new way and to do something about this; you and your reader hope she'll change. She doesn't.

A good story is a work of art. It has shape and meaning. It is unified. Everything in the story contributes to the whole. There are no loose, extraneous parts rattling about.

This is what a story is not: it is not an essay, not an exploration of an idea, although ideas will be present. If you find yourself thinking, Oh, I have this great *idea* about two characters who meet and then they do this or that which will illustrate their existential crises, beware. You're writing to prove a theory rather than writing to discover insights about a character. When we start with a preconceived idea such as this, usually the idea isn't very original. Usually it's been around a while. Many people know about it. If you want to write about ideas, write essays. Literature students, accustomed to discussing themes in fiction, often make the mistake of thinking fiction writers begin with a theme. They don't. In fact, when writers write to illustrate an idea, their characters are forced into saying and doing things to fit into the idea. As a result, the characters are one dimensional, plastic. A story bred of an idea or written to prove a point is doomed.

Here are some other things to avoid as you write stories. Don't pre-plot. Some writers do have a sense of what happens in the end, but they hold their endings in open palms, abandoning them if their characters seem to want to go in other directions. Don't write to show that your character behaves in such and such a way under stress. And don't write to show that, as a result of an experience, your character has become a certain kind of person. Don't decide your characters' fates ahead of time or they'll be flat.

Instead, start with a character in trouble and write in order to find out who she is and what she does. Write with an open mind.

Before you write your first story, remember that you tell stories. Everyone does. You tell stories about your morning commute, your crazy relatives, your computer class, your job, the house that burned next door, your encounter with the police. The trick is to recognize the difference between a story and an anecdote. Here is an anecdote: a woman was invited to a party and she went in a dress that was ridiculous and she felt ridiculous. This anecdote is vague and slight. It lacks a character, a developed conflict and meaning. There are no details that involve us. Virginia Woolf wrote the story beyond the anecdote, and it's called "The New Dress." A woman named Mabel, who is poor, is asked to a party by people who are rich and seem important and glamorous to her. The woman can't afford an expensive dress, so she has a dressmaker create what she hopes will be a charming old-fashioned dress that can compete, by being original, with the expensive, fashionable dresses of the other guests. She arrives at the party, knows at once she's absurd and is forced to review her whole inadequate life. She leaves, defeated. And *this* is a story because a real character experiences a specific conflict; she is complex and we get to know her deeply; something important happens; life will never be exactly the same for her after this party, and the details of the story—the description of the dress, the party, and her thoughts are vivid and involve us in the experience. This story has shape and point and meaning.

Think of the best stories you've heard and told. The characters were probably unique, distinctive, complex; they were engaged in conflict, tension, rising action, a crisis or turning point, falling action, and some kind of resolution. And as you told your story these elements fell into place. Conflict was not something you had to work hard to impose on a story—it *was* the story. You didn't think after the conflict erupted in a crisis, "Oh, now I need falling action." Resolution was not something you pasted on as an afterthought; your story resolved as a result of what had gone on before. As you told the story, you also listened, and you both guided the story and let it guide you.

One of the skills that comes with experience is learning different ways of exploring and revealing main characters, recognizing conflict, playing with it, playing it up and discovering the meaning of what's happening on the page as you write. As you read and write stories, you'll distinguish them from anecdotes, character sketches, prose poems, descriptions, and essays.

You learn what stories are by telling them, listening to them, reading and writing them. Each new story extends your understanding, broadens your definition.

Excercises

1. Read a story you love. Pay attention to how the writer focuses on a character in trouble. See where and how the tension is introduced, mounts, where it erupts in a crisis, how

the story resolves. Notice the details that involve you in the character's experience. Don't be afraid to mark up the story in your book.

2. Tell a story that fascinates you now—a story you've heard, a story you've lived, a family story, a story you might tell your best friend over coffee. Tell the short version as simply and directly as you can.

Ask your listener what she thought was the best part. Ask what details were strong and where she'd like more. Ask if she was confused about anything.

Retell your story. This time emphasize the parts that seemed to work best the first time through, adding detail where appropriate, cutting the weaker parts, clarifying, lying a little or a lot. (Did you lie on the first telling? Are you unable to tell a story without embellishment? Good sign. Fiction writers are professional liars.)

Now, having told your story and having listened to your friend's reaction, do a brief analysis, connecting the parts of one or two of the stories with the following terms:

- *Conflict*: What's the problem from the start?
- *Character*: In what ways has your character been revealed?
- *Rising Action*: In what ways is the problem complicated or deepened as the story progresses?
- *Crisis Point*: Where does the drama come to a head? What's the turning point?
- *Falling Action*: Which details unwind the story?
- *Resolution*: How does your story resolve? What does it mean?

The best stories you've heard and told are, fundamentally, the same as stories in print. Telling stories comes naturally to us. Telling stories with shape and point and meaning takes some practice. And writing them takes more practice still. When you write, forget about creating literature and concentrate on your character who's in trouble. As you write, imagine an audience as eager as a five-year-old at bedtime who begs you to read me a story, read some more, read it again.

◧ How writers find stories, how stories come to writers

THERE MUST BE AS MANY WAYS OF COMING UPON AN IDEA for a story as there are stories. Most writers find that their ideas germinate from material in their lives. We urge you, as most new writers are urged, to fashion stories from your experience.

Some writers have had strong conflicts that seem just right for fiction. A very few writers have said they lifted stories from their lives with almost no distortions. Most of us distort, changing the original events to the point that much of the material is no longer recognizable. Some writers become fascinated by someone they know or have seen briefly or have heard about, and that person becomes a main character. Writers are sometimes told stories that they can turn into fiction. A very few writers say stories present themselves seemingly out of nowhere, almost in their entirety, but this is rare and you mustn't wait for it to happen.

Some writers say a first line of a story comes to them; they write it down, and then a second line comes to them, and so forth. Some writers think of an image then write their way to it, filling in the circumstances surrounding it. Some writers know the end of the story before they know anything else, although they'll hold that end loosely in case their characters need to veer off in another direction.

A number of writers say they place their characters in conflict and then follow them around, recording what they do, see, say, think, and feel.

Many writers—and we believe this is usually the best way—write without knowing the whole story. They write to discover more about characters and their situations, to find out what happens.

Be susceptible to stories. Respect what you notice and think about. You may see a stranger who sniffs, overhear something in a restaurant, get a letter from an old friend or have an experience that gets you thinking about something that happened several years ago; you'll mull over what happened in the past, play with it, and a story may evolve. Rebecca Rule is not an athlete. She's never played organized sports in school. But her daughter has—and Rebecca always wanted to. At a little league game, she heard a coach say, after some unfortunate plays and controversial calls: "There's three kids crying in the dugout." The tension in that line got her thinking "what if": What if the coach is newly divorced? What if she once dated the coach of the other team? Or the umpire? What if the umpire is making bad calls on purpose? What if the father of one of the kids shows up drunk (as one did a few games back)? What if things get ugly? Then: What's really at stake here? What might be at stake? A story began to take shape.

Many writers play "what if." There is even a book of exercises by Pamela Painter and Anne Bernays called *What If*. We recommend it. Let's say you had a fight with your older cousin, whom you've always admired, and afterwards you saw him or yourself or your relationship in a new way. What if that fight had escalated and what if instead of just yelling at each other, you'd begun to push each other around and what if you'd pushed too hard—hauled off and punched him? What if there were only two years between you instead of five so that the relationship between you becomes closer and more important to you or to your main character? Even better, what if the fight is between you and your brother so that the relationship is closer still? This would be good if you have a brother and know the world of brothers. Now the fight can be even more meaningful. Play "what if" in order to find a story, shape it, make it as meaningful as possible for the main character, and bring it close enough to your world so you can write about it with authority.

Here is the birthing process of Susan Wheeler's story, "Grieving," that appeared in *Willow Springs*. Several relatives and friends she loved had died in a period of several months. The story she had been working on felt suddenly irrelevant. She kept going to her desk, but for two weeks couldn't write anything. One morning a friend telephoned to say her mother-in-law was dying of cancer. When Susan returned to her desk she felt a story coming on, knew somehow that it was about a woman getting through a day when she was grieving, and wrote these lines: "I'm scraping sediment from the carburetor bowl of our tractor, pressing my thumb close to the screwdriver point, pushing down and forward against a stubborn chunk of grit. Nothing happens though the screwdriver makes a grating sound." Why that detail? Because that morning she watched her husband clean out a carburetor bowl and that action felt right for her main character. In the story no one died. Instead, a brother tried to commit suicide. Why that choice? Having several relatives die felt unbelievable. One person was enough. And she could imagine how stunned and pained she'd be were anything to happen to her brother.

Try some of the methods of finding stories that we discuss in "Exercises to Get You Started" on page 7. Or try some of these other methods that often help writers. Think of conflicts you've experienced. Stories spring from and move forward because of conflict. Think of a relationship that's filled with conflict. Think of turning points, when you saw someone or something in a new way, positive or negative. Or saw yourself in a new way.

Think of a time when you felt part of something new—the adult world, or a new group in school or at camp or at a new job. Think about times when you've chosen not to join or haven't been allowed to join a group. Think of sexual coming-of-age stories.

Think of the times you've been in trouble and see if you can combine two or three episodes into one and turn it into a story. Failure is an occasion for stories. Have you ever failed at something? Why, and how did it affect you? Think of the things you want to do and can't. Many powerful stories are based on the thwarting of a main character's deepest needs and yearnings. Pay attention to your own yearnings and needs and dreams, and to those of other people.

Almost all of us have several mother/daughter or father/ son or mother/son or father/daughter stories. There are brother, sister, lover, friend, enemy, and roommate stories. There are stories about people in conflict with themselves, with nature, with their ideals or morals, with jobs, sports, school, vacations, hobbies, social groups. Many people have money or housing or health problems. Think of all the things you know how to do: ride the subway, repair a car engine, play pool, play soccer, play the flute, garden, fish, comfort friends in trouble, clean an oven, study (or avoid it), put up with difficult relatives, drink too much, fight, get people mad at you, caulk a boat, live in a camp or a jail.

Before you write, be interested in your main character. You should want to find out more about him. Writing about an experience and a character you understand perfectly won't interest you nearly as much as discovering more about some- one or about a relationship that's complex, critically impor- tant to you, and not fully understood.

Think of experiences your friends have gone through that reverberate deeply for you, that you can identify with. As we discuss in more detail in our chapter on "Inventing Charac- ters," page 65, writers often develop composite characters who are partly themselves and partly one or two other people they know.

Exercises

1. If you can't get going on a story, take some notes. Write in a journal. Do this every day at least two hours a day. Sooner or later a story will come to you. You may have to wait a week, two, three. But wait. Try some exercises, fool around on the

page. Flannery O'Connor said that she always went to her desk even when she couldn't write. Something would come to her—perhaps only one detail, a glimpse of something— and she needed to be at her desk to write it down. That one detail could develop into something larger.

2. If you're stumped for ideas, try lists. List people and experiences that have caused you conflict, troubles you've experienced, failures. List things you know how to do. Think of family relationships and experiences you might write about. List your flaws that have gotten you in trouble. List the flaws of your family and friends. Think about some of these entries, and take notes on the page, playing "what if." See if you can't work one of them into a story.

3. Each day for two weeks write down one hard, harsh truth about yourself and/or someone you know well. These truths will probably be things you would never tell anyone else, perhaps have not yet dared admit to yourself before.

4. Write down a secret you've never told anyone. Write down a secret you know about someone else that he or she wouldn't want you to talk about, perhaps even to know.

5. Summarize the three best short stories you've ever read. Write down what happens in each story. Start with the conflict and then write that this happened and then this and so forth. Often this process can get you going on a story of your own.

6. Keep a small notebook and pen in your hip pocket, and as you go through your days, jot down ideas for stories or interesting characters as they appear in your life and imagination. Some day these may turn into stories.

You have wonderful stories in you, you've heard wonderful stories, and now you're learning to make them up out of all you've seen and heard and lived in your life. There are stories everywhere if we're susceptible. Become susceptible. Go through life with an awareness of small moments and details.

Listen to the stories you hear, improving on them in your own mind, and pay attention to the people whom you think about most often. All of this is material that can be turned into a story if it strikes you in the right way, if you play with it, distort, invent, and write to see what happens.

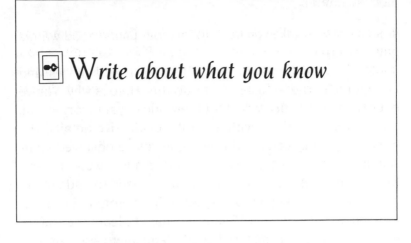

Write about what you know

WRITERS, LIKE MANY PEOPLE, OFTEN WISH THEY CAME FROM backgrounds other than their own: the middle-class suburban woman wants her main character to be a rancher. A man who grew up in a two-room flat longs to write about a middle-class suburban neighborhood. A millionaire wants to write about a bag lady. We know a young man who grew up in northern Maine and wrote about the chairman of the board of a New York advertising company. The new writer didn't know this world and readers smelled rats. The details were second-hand, stale clichés he'd picked up from T.V. and books.

You've probably heard it before, but it's important enough to say again: Write about what you know. When you do you have a much better chance of writing with authority and of convincing readers that your fictional world is true than when you write about unfamiliar worlds.

Like most people, fiction writers have known trouble and conflict. They may have failed at something or been outsiders in school, at love, in social situations, or at their jobs. Maybe their parents had a grueling divorce. Often they know anger, self-pity, fear, shame, discouragement, loss, grief. Their problems have ripened them. The writers have been forced to reflect, to try to make sense of what's happened, and this has resulted in their knowing things about people and relationships, has given them an understanding that others may lack.

Your experiences, your family, or social background may have caused you pain, but this pain can be turned into fine stories. Often it takes courage to face our pasts; good writers have courage.

Most new writers write from their own experiences and backgrounds, and we urge you to do this. Here is why. You've got to convince your reader that the world of your story is real. You do that by writing with accurate, distinctive details. The most convincing details will be those you've observed your-self. If you use sloppy, canned details, readers won't believe what happens. Another reason is that you need to understand your own life before you can expect to have profound insights into other characters. And finally, it's hard to learn the craft of fiction. So learn on material that's familiar to you. As you write a dramatic scene, you'll learn more quickly, more suc-cessfully how to get inside a character's head, to write good dialogue, to summarize time, and so forth, if you're describing a world you know than if you have to imagine a place you never visited. Later you can depart from your background and experiences.

Some new writers feel their worlds are too ordinary to be interesting. This is nonsense. Think of Sherwood Anderson, who grew up in an ordinary midwestern town and wrote sto-ries placed in that setting. Many of them were collected in his book, *Winesburg, Ohio*. He drew on people he knew and the world he knew, distorting, of course. The best writers trust their territories. You must, too.

You probably know a lot about being a son or a daughter, a brother or sister, about living in a family of some kind, about being a student, a roommate, a lover. Maybe you know about being a spouse, somebody's mother or father or grandmother, being a member of a chess team or a political action group. You may know a lot about fishing, stealing, or losing or win-ning at poker, fist fights, or love. You may know what it's like to drive with a bus load of students to hockey games, what it's like to be excluded from games on a school yard, or to be asked or not asked to parties you want to go to. You may know what it's like to have your heart broken or to be passive or aggressive, moody, drunk, unreasonable, or courageous. You may know what it's like to be a Catholic or Jew or Hindu, or a

Chinese-American or Spanish-American or African-American. Characters with strong religious and/or cultural backgrounds can enrich stories. You may know what it is to have grown up in a trailer or a house on the ocean with a swimming pool, or a room in an inner city, or a split-level house in a suburban development. Certainly you know, as everyone knows, the strong feelings that are the core of fiction: love, hate, fear, joy, pride, anger, discouragement, determination, shame, success, jealousy, envy, greed, competition, grief. Everyone has experienced these emotions. That's why we love to read about other people's experiences with them.

So in your early stories, resist the urge to write about emotions, relationships, places, and territories that are unfamiliar to you. Trust, as all good writers trust, that your world and experiences are worth writing about. And write about them.

Exercises

1. In your journal, list your territories: places, activities, jobs, worlds you know well. Write as fast as you can, jotting down even absurd sounding things, such as talking to your roommate as you brush your teeth at adjoining sinks in the bathroom.

These are areas of authority, useful in determining where to set your stories, what your characters do, what they think about, what they know.

Take a sheet of paper and list ideas for stories that emerge from the territories. You may be surprised when an idea for a story springs from brushing your teeth. Be as cryptic as you like. Let associations flow. When you think of baking pies, you might think of raking blueberries with your family on Parker Mountain. You might think of your brother, as a teenager, and the awful thing he said about your best friend. You might think about how your mother-in-law over sweetens everything. Any of these associations may be the kernel of a story.

Save the list. Add to it from time to time.

2. List the relationships that have caused conflict for you. They should still be unresolved in some way, should nag at you. You'll likely have a story here.

3. List all the emotions you can think of on two pieces of paper. Leave spaces between words. In those spaces, list people or experiences you associate with each emotion. Again, free associate. There will probably be one person's name that appears frequently and you may find yourself writing about her or him.

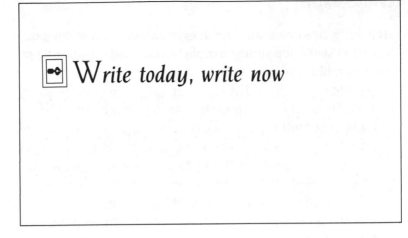

Write today, write now

DON'T WAIT FOR A BRILLIANT STORY IDEA TO COME ALONG.

Don't wait until you know exactly what's going to happen, who your characters are, how long the story will be, and where it will probably be published.

Don't wait until you've read one hundred stories by the best writers in the world so you know what a good story is and you've witnessed one thousand useful techniques for producing one.

Write now, and see what happens.

If you're holding back, ask yourself, "What's the worst that can happen?"

Take the risk.

Exercises

1. Find a very short story you love. Model a story of your own after it.

2. Write a survival story. In "The Good Humor Man," Rebecca Morris writes about a woman who feels devastated after her husband tells her he wants a divorce. In the story we learn how she survives. The conflict is stated in the first line: "All through that hot, slow summer, I lived alone, on ice-cream sandwiches and gin, in a one-room apartment on Carmine Street, waiting while James divorced me." She follows him around like a detective, then gives that up and begins, step by

step, to live her own life. In the end, she is locking arms with two other swimmers, doing a triple flip off the diving board into the water. She has learned to trust her swimming partners and to execute perfect flips. The story ends with the narrator saying that the summer is over and she has kept her head.

Think of something that has devastated you or a character you want to write about. Know the character's world so you can be specific. Assume the devastating event has already taken place. State the conflict at once. And write to find out how, over a period of a day, a week, or a couple of months, your character survives or fails to survive. Try to keep the story under five pages.

3. Write a decision story. James Joyce's "Eveline" is only three pages long and it's about a decision. Model a story after this. In the Joyce story, the main character has to decide whether to run away with her boyfriend to Buenos Aires or to stay home where she will continue to be mistreated by her father and by her boss. Eveline thinks about her life at home, and her love for her boyfriend. She decides to stay at home.

When you write your story about a character facing a critically important life decision, don't plan ahead of time what she'll decide. Discover what she thinks and feels and how she sees her world. Find out what happens. Keep the story under five pages.

4. Write a story like Ernest Hemingway's "Hills Like White Elephants"—one that is mostly dialogue and that takes place over a short period of time (a few minutes, an hour). Describe the setting briefly and in a way that reveals character. Use the way the characters see or use objects to show tension.

Whether these stories turn out to be strong or weak, worth revising or worth a good laugh, you've walked your way through the process. You've created characters, put them in conflict, seen how they interact. Something has happened. Life is not exactly the same anymore.

You've probably been surprised by some of the things your characters have thought or said or done. You've probably noticed that what they see and how they regard what they see affects them and the story. You've probably noticed how much your characters' reactions to objects and setting can reveal, and noticed how fast dialogue fills a page how it can move a story forward or slow it down. You've probably written some parts that aren't needed, perhaps some clichés that you can cut in the next draft, should there be one. You've probably written at least one line you like.

You've written a story. You can learn from this. Your next story will be better for your having written this one.

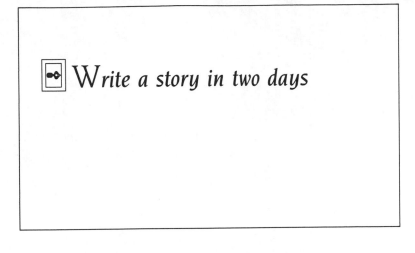

Write a story in two days

TRY THIS: WRITE A STORY IN TWO DAYS. KNOWING YOU HAVE only two days will free you; the story can't be perfect. That's not the point, not at all. This is an exercise, like playing the scales on a piano. You'll have the experience of writing quickly, of seeing again the elements of a story. You'll write a story that has a beginning, a middle, and an end. You'll focus on your main character, who is in trouble, and after the crisis or revelation, life for him won't be exactly the same anymore.

Before you do this assignment, read four or five very short stories and concentrate on structure. How are the main characters and conflicts introduced? How do the conflicts mount and finally erupt? Pay attention to pacing—the movement of the stories.

And then write, telling yourself that this is only an exercise, a chance to fool around. It mustn't become a test of your talent. If you feel it will turn into one, stop. If you show it to someone (and probably you shouldn't), the person mustn't critique it. Probably you won't want to revise it. But the fact that you've written a story in two days, rough as it necessarily will be, is wonderful.

PROCESS

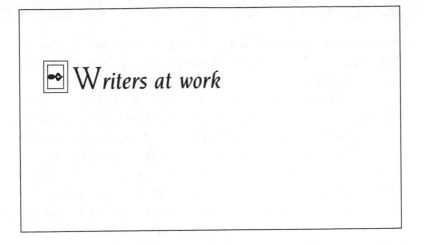

Writers at work

PROCESS VARIES FROM WRITER TO WRITER, FROM STORY TO story, so we won't discuss *a* process or *the* process, but process possibilities—some methods by which writers find their ways into stories and through them.

Usually a story happens in stages, many of which overlap: from conception and gestation when a small detail or a character or a whole story takes hold and grows in your mind, to that first birthing draft, and on through many revisions to the final nitpicky editing. Many of these stages are covered in detail throughout the book.

Conception

Some stories may come from a glimmer of something that excites or puzzles or nags at you; perhaps you don't know why. The glimmer could be a smear of lipstick on someone's teeth, a piece of conversation you overheard, the smell of oil in a garage, or lilies at a funeral. Or something may happen that strikes a deep chord, reminding you of a past experience.

Conception can be a delicate, elusive, tender stage in the writing process. Other times a character or story idea will come to you suddenly and fill you to bursting. There are writers who go around with a number of characters in their heads; whoever makes the most noise, gets on the page.

You may have carried some experiences around with you for years. Very likely, they are bred of conflict that is not fully resolved. Through writing, you'll gain understanding even though you'll distort what happened in order to make your story work. We don't mean "distort" in a negative way here, but events are changed in fiction in order to fit with the larger whole and larger truth that is the story. Sometimes writers will take events that almost happened in their lives and make them happen on the page. Often a writer becomes fascinated by a person, wants to know her more fully, and so he writes. Writers often write about themselves because they need more understanding. Perhaps most often, our characters are composites of many people we know, ourselves included. Some stories come from a yearning or nostalgia for something missed. Some come from the writer's need to understand a life he'd never know or understand unless he wrote about it.

Quick notes in your journal can help you hold on to a glimmer, identify a chord. Record story ideas, however briefly, when they come, because they may not come again.

Gestation

The gestation period may last a few minutes or years. Many writers wait several years before writing about a personal experience, believing they need objectivity. Others can return from a train trip and write about it the next day.

Some writers tell of stories that appear almost in their entirety all at once in their heads. Shirley Jackson wrote "The Lottery" in one draft at one morning work session. This is rare. Don't wait for this kind of inspiration: you're likely to go to the grave before it comes.

Gestation may involve turning a character over in your mind from time to time as you might turn over an interesting stone in your hands. You may stare at the blank pages or at your computer screen for hours, days, even weeks, thinking hard about your characters and stories before you're ready to begin.

Journals provide a place for gestation to occur. When a writer mulls over a question or a problem on the page, a story may emerge.

First draft

Some writers write a first sentence containing a piece of information that fascinates them; that leads to another sentence, then to another. Some begin with a character in trouble and write to see what happens.

Writers often start with a conflict in mind. Get a hint of conflict going in your first paragraph. Conflict will make you want to write to find out what happens, and make readers want to keep turning your pages.

Some writers explore their stories in a journal, jotting down notes until they sense it's time to begin; others say if they did this they'd understand too much and lose the motivation to write. Most writers don't discuss stories in process, especially early on, because talk sucks the juice out.

Many writers find if they know the ending ahead of time, they'll force their characters toward that preconception; the characters will be flat and the story contrived. Some writers need the security of knowing where they're headed in their stories, but they're wise enough to keep these plans tentative, abandoning their preconceptions when the stories take unexpected turns.

You will find your way. You will find a way to write that makes sense and that feels right for your story. Then you'll experiment with another method in the next.

The important thing is to write that first draft. Get the story on your pages, no matter how rough. Many writers rush through jotting a few words for a section they know they'll want to expand later, anything to get the story down, however skeletal, while they're hot.

This horrifies a few writers who believe each word must be honest and exact. These writers explore each moment fully along the way, one moment leading to the next. They don't understand how writers can know what happens next unless the previous moment is fully developed. Some writers start with a burst of energy, then slow down, agonize over what happens next for several writing sessions, then experience another burst. Others plod along fairly steadily.

Many new writers, determined to get it right the first time and committed to efficiency, will be so persnickety with each sentence they'll give themselves writer's block.

Our advice is: Get the first draft down as quickly as you can. Then go back.

The first draft is for you. Tape above your computer screen or work table during first drafts: This draft is for me. No Critics Allowed.

The first draft is exploratory. Novelist, journalist, columnist, poet, and teacher Don Murray compares writers to explorers going through unmarked territory. Some writers compare themselves to deep sea divers, diving down again and again, peering with flashlights, poking about, feeling their ways along. They come up many times with lots of seaweed and mud before they find the treasure.

As you write your early drafts, be playful, as children are when they build sand castles: they have no thought of "right" or "wrong," no critics whispering in their ears, "This is dumb," or "Why bother." A child gladly pulls down a turret she's built, makes a newer, larger one, then smashes the whole structure because she's decided to build a fort. Children know how to enjoy the creative process; many writers do, too.

Some writers speak of the terror of facing the blank page. Many say writing is painful, even agonizing—and there is pain in revelation, or in the frustration when what's in your head is not on the page, or in how damn long the process takes and how hard it is. Most writers love to get together with other writers to moan and groan from time to time. But writing is also play. It's playing with a character, discovering who he or she is; it's imagining. It's fascinating, infuriating, frustrating, depressing, and fun. Most writers say it gives them a satisfaction that nothing else does.

Revision

Don't be discouraged by rough early drafts. As you revise, you can get to know your characters, portray them well, discover and explore conflicts, grope toward resolution, and refine your language.

Some writers say they start red hot and revise until they're cold and critical. In those first few drafts, it's probably best not to be too self-critical. You'll become increasingly aware of your readers and their needs as you revise, until by the final draft, you'll be reading as an editor or as an objective reader.

But don't think if you've written one or two drafts you are done. Our advice is: Revise, revise, revise. Raymond Carver said he's done twenty or thirty drafts of a story, and never fewer than ten or twelve drafts. This is not unusual. Re-vision is the chance to see again, see more deeply, fully, clearly. As we rewrite, we gradually come to know our characters more fully, to know what our story is really about. Many writers revise as they go along, reworking the pages they wrote a day or several days before, then writing new material. In our guide on revising on page 217 we discuss in detail problems writers face in revision.

After you finish draft one, you may want to let the writing cool for several days, or a week or two, and work on something else. This will give you distance. Some writers, though, can't bear to leave a piece once started.

If you've sketched in scenes, one of your primary tasks in revision will be to flesh them out. We call this internal expansion. You may know where your story begins and ends after the first draft, but you'll need to fill in the details, bring the scenes to life with more description, probe characters with more dialogue or thought, fill in the blanks with narration. The story will grow longer as you expand internally.

Often after expansion, you'll want to cut. Having written ten fine sensuous details to bring your readers into your main character's living room, you may decide you've overdone it, and cut away all but the best three. Having written two scenes showing a character's violent temper, you may decide that one will suffice.

Don't be afraid to throw a whole draft out and start over. Professional writers fill garbage cans with paper for each story. It's usually new writers who are reluctant to begin again or make large changes. Our attitude is that nothing is wasted in this process. The scene or section we throw away has helped us to understand our characters and story. The draft thrown out teaches us how to write the next by showing us what not to do. Each draft informs the next, even if not one word is carried forward.

In revision you'll come to understand more about what your story means. You may know that this happens and then this and then this, but what do these events mean? What's the theme? You'll discover the meaning along the way, and by the final draft you'll make sure everything in the story contributes to that theme.

If you've lost faith in your story (and sometimes this happens) ask yourself these questions: Do you tend to be a quitter and do you need to stick with this story or risk losing it forever? Or do you need to put it aside, perhaps coming back to it weeks or years from now when you can decide whether to rework or abandon it? Some new writers fail to persevere, thinking their stories are unworthy, when in fact they are merely unfinished.

The ability and determination to revise is often what separates writers who publish from those who don't. Persevere. Do justice to your character, your story.

Nitpick editing

Make each word right. Be clear. Include the reader: your reader must see. When your character crosses the field we want to know whether he runs, walks, or stumbles. We want to know if the wind in your story is a hurricane or a gale, whether your main character loves or likes her roommate, whether it's cold or cool. Words matter. Much of your rewriting will be making the words exact. When your writing is accurate, you have authority. Your readers will trust you and believe your story. When your writing is sloppy, readers will mistrust you.

Writers use punctuation to clarify and modify. For instance, a semicolon connects two sentences more closely than if the first were to end in a period. A comma makes the reader pause. A dash at the end of a line of dialogue can show that the speaker was interrupted; ellipses would show that the speaker trailed off.

In a four-thousand-word story, a professional writer will, by the last draft, be able to justify the four thousand word choices as well as hundreds of decisions about punctuation, sentence structure, and paragraphing.

Your stories deserve this attention, too.

As you write, notice your writing methods. Which methods work for you and which don't? If you're writing well, don't change your method, but if after a week you're unable to write even one page because you're trying too hard to get each word right as you go along, try something else. Know your weaknesses, too. If you tend not to finish things, you may want to make a pact with yourself that you'll finish a draft of this story you're working on even if it's horrible.

Exercise

Read a few interviews from the series *Writers at Work: The Paris Interviews*. In these, published writers talk about their writing methods and habits, their joys and frustrations, their views of literature. There are other collections, such as interviews of women and African-American writers. Reading these can comfort and inspire you, make you feel part of a community of writers.

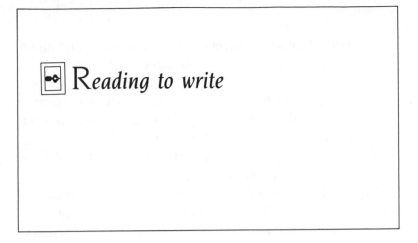

Reading to write

MOSTLY, YOU'LL LEARN TO WRITE BY WRITING. AND REVISING.

You'll also learn a great deal by reading. We said this in "Letter to a New Writer," and we can't stress it enough: writers learn much of the craft by studying published stories and absorbing ideas and techniques.

Often as you read a story—let's say you just read one about falling in love—you'll think of a story of your own that needs telling. Don't worry that your story about love may already have been told or that a technique you've adopted will seem like theft. Your experience, your particular view of the world from your particular place in it should ensure that your story will be different and will bear your thumb print.

Find stories you love. If you're like most people, you'll learn the most from writers you love. Get some good, fat anthologies and start reading first pages. (For a long list of recommended books and stories, see page 269.) If, at the end of page one, you like a story, read on. If you don't, go to another story. When you find a writer whose work fascinates you, consider making that writer your mentor for a while. Go to a library and read a collection or two of her stories. Become immersed in that writer's work. When you've learned what you need to, find another mentor.

Read a favorite story again and again to learn how it works. Stop every time you come to a scene, a paragraph, a sentence that you think is wonderful; read it several times; ask yourself what novelist Carolyn Chute asks herself as she reads: "How did the writer *do* that?" Then read the passage again and figure out how. After this process, the skill or technique will become yours to use in your fiction. This kind of scrutiny—holding a magnifying glass to the page—is a fascinating way to read stories, and you'll be joining the community of writers who, for years, have stolen one another's tricks.

Read the same story every night before you go to bed for a week. You'll absorb techniques by osmosis.

You may have had literature courses where you discussed themes and symbols. For now, put these concerns away. Now, you must read as a writer: to learn the trade. Let's pretend for a moment we are carpenters and we're standing beside several art historians, all of us looking at a beautiful chair made by Lee Wong. We all admire the lovely curves of the legs. Several of the art historians talk about the clear influence of an earlier furniture maker on Wong. Very likely they discuss Wong's place in the history of carpentry—a valid, interesting conversation. But we are carpenters. We place our hands on that chair, turn it upside down, examine whether the legs are glued to the base of the chair or nailed, and we figure out exactly how the arm is made to fit into the back of the chair. We must know these things because we need to build chairs; if we pay close attention, we will learn skills to apply to our work. Like carpenters, writers turn stories upside down.

Know your writing weaknesses and read to cure them. Say you've had trouble beginning your stories; you tend to start slowly, failing to launch the conflict or tension right away. Read the first paragraph or two of fifteen short stories in an anthology, one right after another.

Some writers learn by typing out a few stories of their favorite published writers. By typing one sentence after another, they scrutinize craft. They feel they're inside the published writer's mind, seeing the world as the published writer does, making decisions along with him, becoming aware of each word.

Type at least one story by a writer whose work you love. Write favorite paragraphs or sentences in a notebook. Read these over from time to time.

Here are some things to study as you read: Where and how is the conflict or tension introduced and how does the writer keep it mounting all through? When does the conflict erupt? What happens as a result of the crisis? How is the main character presented and developed? In what ways does the writer reveal character? Does the writer get inside the main character's head and, if so, how does he show the person's thoughts and feelings, then pull back and let readers *see* what's going on? Does the writer stay inside the main character's head for long passages or just short ones, or both?

Pay attention to how writers rely on details, using the five senses, especially sight. What are the best details? Are there a few or a lot of adjectives? Is there a dominant impression of people and places that's given right away when they're first introduced? Does the writer tend to write full, rich, rather long descriptions like William Faulkner, Gabriel García Márquez, Toni Morrison, Alice Munro, Katherine Anne Porter and Eudora Welty?

Or is this a bare-bones writer, a taker-outer-of-details like Ernest Hemingway, Joan Didion, Ann Beattie, and Raymond Carver? Read one story by a taker-outer, then right away, another by a putter-inner. Throughout the story, does the writer comment on what happens or are only the surface events recorded? How does the story begin and end? What if it began another way, at another point in time; how would that affect the story? Are there flashbacks, and, if so, how does the writer go back in time, then return to the heart of the story without confusing the reader? How does the material in the flashback section add to the burden of the main character and push the story ahead? Who tells the story? A first person narrator ("I")? Or is it third person ("she" or "he")? How does the writer get characters from the kitchen to the bedroom, from Paris to New York without boring or confusing the reader? How is time handled? If a two- or three-minute period of time is important to the story, how does the writer stress that moment? How does the writer get from Tuesday night to Wednesday morning, and how does she summarize several years? What makes you want to keep turning those pages?

What does the story mean? What is its theme, and how is it operating all through? Do you think the writer made a mistake in any part of the story? Remember that you're a story writer, too, and you can spot places where a story may not work for you.

If you're having trouble with a technique, read writers who handle it particularly well. Let's say you have trouble revealing your main characters' feelings and thoughts. You'd be helped by studying many writers, including Margaret Atwood, Toni Cade Bambara, Anton Chekhov, Andre Dubus, Alice Munro, John Updike, and Virginia Woolf, who often go into their characters' minds in short phrases as well as in long passages, and sometimes even for pages or for the whole story.

Some writers like to read from work they despise. It makes them realize how much better *they* write.

Know your cultural, economic, geographical, social, philosophical and/or spiritual backgrounds and leanings; read from writers who've written stories placed in these categories. You'll pick up ideas from these writers that will help you express your characters' views and experiences.

It's important, too, to read from backgrounds different from yours: as you explore differences, light will be shed on your experiences. Read also, stories written by the old masters such as Flaubert and Chekhov. We need to know what earlier writers wrote about and how they solved problems. Why reinvent the wheel? Read an anthology that includes some of their work as well as stories by writers up through the present.

You can learn a lot by reading a textbook or two on writing fiction, remembering that writers sometimes disagree about fiction—and that's all right.

Exercises

1. Read anthologies until you find a writer whose work you love. Then read more of that writer's work.

2. Discuss specific stories with another fiction writer. Mark the stories up and teach each other what you've learned about craft.

3. Read favorite passages aloud to yourself and, later, to a friend. When you read aloud you both see and hear the words, so the impact is stronger. Have others read passages to you.

4. Type at least three pages of a story you love written by a published writer. This exercise may sound strange to you, but we think you'll gain so much from the close scrutiny that you'll type the rest of the story.

For some reason, many new writers tend to underestimate how much they can teach themselves by studying published stories, and so we say again: read, scrutinize stories, and learn from them.

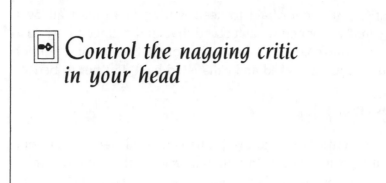

Control the nagging critic in your head

MOST WRITERS HAVE NAGGING CRITICS WHOSE VOICES CAN sometimes get so loud and destructive that the writers can't write. Here are some things inner critics like to say: This stinks! Who cares? Your grammar is terrible. You always were a bore and this is boring too. You're so damned slow at writing, and this is so hard to do, you might as well clean out the garage and write later. Face it, you lack talent and brains. Why don't you quit writing and become an accountant?

Each of us must control his own critic. Tell your critic to go away for now. Later, you will ask her back when she can help you with spelling and grammar, and check to see if you've developed your scenes enough, or if you need to delve more deeply into your main character. It's important to assure the critic that she will be of use later. That way, she'll go away more readily when she isn't needed.

Most internal critics fear failure. They are crippled by this fear. They would never have the courage to dive into stories not knowing what might happen next.

Natalie Goldberg in *Writing Down the Bones* suggests that writers buy a goofy notebook—one with shiny-maroon and bilious-green cartoon characters or pink gorillas on the cover. This is called a No Critics Allowed Book. The cover will be so silly and childish that you can write anything you want in it. No one will see, no one will judge. It's that childish state you often need to return to as you write, so that you can play with raw material, fool around, and see what happens. Unlike the critic, you're not afraid to keep writing or to start all over again. The poor critic can't stand that kind of uncertainty, just hasn't the spirit to tolerate exploring the unknown. Poor thing. She's panicked and exhausted by it. Put her to bed.

Exercise

If your critic won't go away when you tell her to, put your writing aside for fifteen minutes, and let the critic dictate a letter to you. She will use your name, "Dear Danielle" or "Dear Sol." Let the critic say every rotten thing about you she's ever thought or said. Don't worry about logic or fairness. Just turn the critic loose on the page. Then, when you read the letter out loud, you'll be astonished at how vindictive, illogical and downright absurd she is. Hopefully you'll laugh. Finally, as if you were your own best, most supportive friend, write that critic a letter pointing out where she's unreasonable and wrong. Tell her you're trying to write and that takes courage. You're exploring on the page, groping, feeling your way along. This draft and probably the next three to six drafts are for you, not her. You need to discover things about your main character and to see what she will do, think, say, and feel. Remind your critic that critics only criticize finished products. They come in after your hard work is done.

What to do
when you're stumped

YOUR CHARACTERS ARE HAPPY—TOO HAPPY. YOUR CHARACTERS are miserable—sodden with misery. Your characters are standing around in somebody's living room drinking wine or smoking cigarettes, talking, eating crackers, coughing, shifting their weight from foot to foot. Nothing is happening. Nothing has been happening for several pages. You're stumped.

Leave your story for a day or two. Then reread it, asking yourself: What is this story about? Where is it going? When you're stumped, the problem usually lies before the place you stopped writing. Often it has to do with lack of a clear conflict. Maybe you haven't gone deeply enough into your characters earlier and you need to go back and learn more about them. Are there enough good details so that, as you wrote, you learned about who your characters were? Did you get side-tracked?

Go back to the last strong, honest sentence that you wrote, a sentence you have confidence in. Cut everything after it and continue your story from that sentence.

Ask yourself if you really care about this character and if her situation is critically important to her, and to you.

Or you can try introducing a new element.

Have a new character come into the room. Let the telephone ring. Maybe sparks fly out of the fireplace and set somebody's socks on fire. Maybe lightning strikes a tree just outside the window.

See how these people react. See what happens.

With almost every story, you'll feel stumped some time in the process. You'll come to a point where you just can't bear to work on it any more. You'll think it is a terrible story. Or just a mediocre story. Or you don't care much about the characters anymore. Or, and this happens a lot, you've come to the really hard going. You'll have interesting characters in an interesting situation, but you're just not sure where to go from here; you're afraid if you force your way through to an ending, you'll trivialize or contrive or seek easy answers in your push to get through.

Try leaving the story for a few weeks. Let it sit. Work on something else. Come back to it when it draws you back, because all of a sudden you've got an idea or you're thinking of a scene you know you want to revise or you realize something about one of your characters.

Try showing your story to a good reader. Ask specific questions about elements of the story that concern you. (Is it too long? Do I need that scene on page 5? Does Maggie seem too mean? And: What do you think this story is about? And: What characters, scenes, passages need to be stronger?)

Try the internal expansion technique that we described in our guide "Controlling Time." Try line-by-line editing. Tell yourself you're going back over the story just once more to sharpen every detail, to make sure each sentence is honest. Begin at the beginning, reading aloud, slowly. Is every word right? Is the punctuation working well? Listen for the rhythms of the sentences; play around with those rhythms as you tighten. And while you're working on the sentence level, add sensuous detail, make the scenes fuller, more complete, try to see your fictional world with absolute clarity. You may discover tensions in scenes that you didn't know were there; you may learn about your characters; you may discover meaning in the smallest details.

Here's another stumper: you've been working on a story for a while. You love, for example, the scene between Harriet and the toothless man at the corner grocery store; you love certain passages; you think Harriet is a well-developed character. The story should be working. But it's not. Something is wrong. Any of the exercises above may help. Or you might start again. Put the old draft out of sight.

Start your story over without referring to any of your previous drafts. You will remember the best material and forget the rest. You may discover possibilities that you couldn't see in the old draft because you were too fond of it.

Try writing the same story but make a big change, shake it up. Change the time frame. Instead of writing about six months of her life, write about three weeks, or one night. Change the point-of-view character. Instead of writing from the point of view of the teacher, write from the point of view of his wife or a child, or the school principal, or the nurse down the hall who has a crush on him. Change the point of view from first person to third (with the same point-of-view character). Or experiment with second person or omniscient. Change the tense. A story written in present tense is very different from the same one in past tense. Try changing the tense in just a few paragraphs at first, to see the extent of the transformation.

What if you can't seem to make any headway in a story? You're stumped from the beginning. You have a small idea; maybe a note in your journal that seems to have potential, or maybe you have no idea at all. It's writing time and you're not writing. You're staring at a blank page or a blank computer screen. You think you're caught writer's block.

Time yourself. Get the kitchen timer, set it to twenty minutes and just write. Write anything at all—even gibberish— but write. When the bell goes off, if you can bear it, set the timer for another twenty minutes and write again. Usually the third twenty-minute sequence is the charm. You've been writing for an hour, and if you can write for an hour, chances are there is something useable on the page or screen. Start your story with that good line or paragraph, or if you're lucky, even more.

If you're working on a computer and if even with the timer you have a hard time writing, because your internal critic keeps telling you how worthless and silly your words are, try turning the screen off and just typing. If your critic can't see your words, he can't criticize them. After a while, when your curiosity demands, you'll print out what you've written or you'll light up the screen.

What if you're stumped not just by one story, but by the whole process of writing fiction? You feel you can't write fiction anymore because it is too hard. Maybe you've just finished a wonderful story, and you know you'll never be able to write another one as good, so why bother? Or your last three stories have been too much alike. All set in a city apartment, all about marriages in trouble, all somewhat depressing. You sit down to write a new story and you can't write; you just don't want to.

Write an essay or a poem or a letter to the editor. Write in your journal. Write about writing. Write something funny or sarcastic or sentimental. If any of these efforts turn into fiction, that's great. If not, you've maintained your writer's discipline, kept your writing muscles in shape, and maybe written a fine essay or poem or letter to the editor.

Imitate. Pick a favorite story by a favorite writer and imitate it. Try writing in present tense like Bobbie Ann Mason. Try repetition of key elements like Tim O'Brien in "The Things They Carried." Try revealing the complexities of a relationship like Flannery O'Connor in "Everything That Rises Must Converge." Imitate form, style, voice, dialect, sentence length, punctuation. Imitate the absurdity of Woody Allen. Incorporate myths like Amy Tan in *The Joy Luck Club*. Immerse your characters in sensuous detail like Gloria Naylor.

Imitate your favorite writers to learn their techniques. You may find originality in imitation.

Find a new place to write. Go to the library, a restaurant, a train station. If you write on a computer, buy a felt-tip marker and a pad of paper and write on that for a while. Break free of your old habits.

Read aloud passages of stories you love and that will inspire you.

Find a poorly written story or book, a piece of prose you hate. Read a page or two and tell yourself, "I can do better than that."

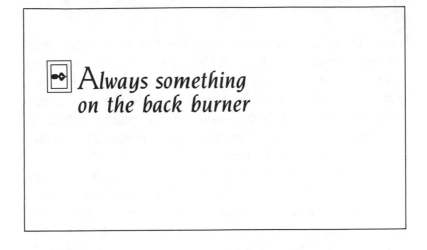

Always something on the back burner

TRY THIS TO ORGANIZE YOUR WORK AND KEEP IT MOVING.

Buy a journal—bound, spiral, large, pocket-sized, cloth-covered, leathery, whatever appeals. This will be for warm-up writing, exercises, quotes, newspaper cutouts, process commentary, and anything else you find helpful. This will be your idea book, never far from your side. This you will write in every day, a little or a lot, depending on how well the stories themselves are going. (When a story takes off for some writers, their journal entries get short and cryptic. When they hit rough going, they may do more journal work; it helps them find their way.)

Also, buy a three ring binder. Black with two-inch rings. No—it doesn't have to be black. It doesn't have to have two-inch rings; one-and-one-half-inchers will do. Buy several dividers for the binder. Each section will hold a story-in-progress. A story-in-progress might be one promising line on top of a blank page. It might be several drafts of a story. It might be the first page, one scene, a dialogue, character notes, or a description of an interesting clay pot. It might be an ending you want to write your way to sometime soon.

Each section holds material you can pick up and work on or from. For some people, the binder eases the pressure, just a little: if this story doesn't quite work out, take heart, there are others on the back burner.

For years, Rebecca Rule worked on one story at a time, hammering them out over a three- to six-week period. Sometimes they turned out well and she felt happy. But, after writing a good story, she found it difficult to start a new one. Each start seemed inferior to the story she'd just finished. Sometimes her stories turned out badly and she felt discouraged. After writing an awful story, she also found it difficult to start on a new one—for fear the new one would be equally awful and not worth the effort.

Some writers hate being between stories. Some work on stories longer than they need to, just to delay entrance into that frightening, empty place between stories where confidence can drain away. Some writers fear they'll never have another idea. They'll never write again, or, even if they do write again, they'll never write anything decent again, that's for sure.

Keeping a journal means you always have bits and pieces to look at, possibilities for something new and promising. Working in the three-ring binder means you have more than one story going at a time. Each day you can choose which story to work on, or your can work on more than one at a sitting, switching gears when you need to.

Ultimately, you'll spend more time with each story. Some will incubate while others will learn to walk.

CHARACTERS

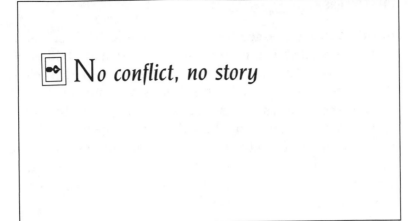

No conflict, no story

ROBERT PENN WARREN SAID IT. WE AGREE.

Start with conflict. Often the conflict will be hidden, more a tension than an outright clashing. Get that conflict going in the first paragraph. Keep the conflict mounting until it erupts in a crisis. Then let readers see the resolution.

Conflict is energy. It is tension. Starting with a character in conflict will give you enthusiasm for writing. You will want to find out what happens next, how the character reacts to this specific conflict, to its complications, to the growing intensity. Your own curiosity and interest in people in trouble will pull you forward into the story—as it will your reader.

Even better, as you focus on a character in trouble, the character will start informing *you* about what happens. He'll do and say things that surprise, horrify, shame, or delight you, as he copes or fails to cope. In conflict, people are revealed more than in harmony.

Conflict can be external: will she survive the hurricane? Or internal: how will he reconcile himself to being jilted? Or it can be both: the kleptomaniac tries to control herself, goes into a store as a kind of test, steals, and is caught.

Often conflict has to do with a character trait or a flaw. For instance, a businessman has a drinking problem and a brutal temper. He manages to keep these problems hidden from his business associates, but his family and neighbors know. The story opens with this as a given, long-term conflict. His wife knows, though he does not, that the new neighbors are best friends with a top executive in the businessman's firm, and that the executive has been invited to a neighborhood pool party on Saturday. The story takes place at the party, which the businessman insists on attending. What happens?

Or this conflict: A seventeen-year-old girl has a mother who remarries a younger man. The girl is of an age where she's naturally flirtatious with men. The stepfather seems to be getting too close to her. All of this will be told in a flashback. When the story opens, the mother has just left them alone for the weekend. What happens?

Exercises

1. Think of two or three conflicts that reverberate deeply for you. Then write a story from one of them.

2. Read several stories looking specifically at conflict. When is conflict introduced? Is there more than one conflict? How do the conflicts mount and connect with one another? Reread the first page and the last. How do the events (or thoughts or comments) on the last page resolve the problems suggested on the first? Or do they?

When you begin with conflict or tension, you begin with energy, action, and, most importantly, the potential for character and plot development. Conflict is the blood of your story. It warms it, feeds it, energizes it. If the conflict engages you, it will engage your readers as well.

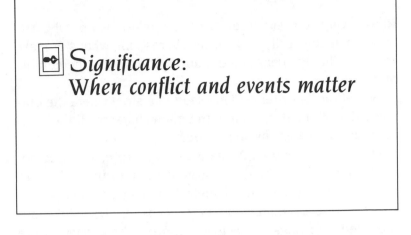

Significance:
When conflict and events matter

SOMETIMES AS STORIES DEVELOP THEY WILL SEEM SLIGHT or trivial. When this happens resist the temptation to impose some unbelievable, flashy action that is not character-based. Don't interject a murder, rape, suicide, fist fight, bombing, or religious conversion in hopes of livening up a story, or to end one because you can't think of a good ending.

Action must spring from character, from who your character is and what she wants and how she is being thwarted. Events and actions imposed on characters make the story seem contrived. Readers will stop believing and the story will fail.

Significance does not lie in what happens externally nearly as much as it lies in what happens within characters. Concentrate on the reverberations. What is at stake for your main character? What does the event mean to her? If an event matters to her (whether she knows it or not), it will matter to the reader.

In some stories, what happens may seem slight at first, but the reverberations are actually profound. In Peter Taylor's story "The Gift of the Prodigal," this is what happens: The main character looks out the window and sees his grown son Ricky standing in the driveway. He speculates about why Ricky has come to see him. Several pages later Ricky comes into the house and they talk.

That's it. But in the process of speculation, observation, memory, and the beginnings of a conversation, the main character and the reader come to understand the significance of

Ricky's visit, the significance of the relationship, who the main character really is, what motivates him, what's at stake for him. What happens emotionally in the story is memorable and dramatic.

Sometimes a writer gets involved in a story where the outcome doesn't matter much to the main character. If the character doesn't care, why should we?

Here's an exception: A character *ought* to care about doing his job well at a hardware store. He's in trouble, about to be fired. He senses this vaguely but doesn't grasp it. He starts out to rearrange the paint cans on the shelf, but the telephone rings. He begins counting the money in the cash register. Then a customer comes in and he puts the money away intending to count it later. Will he finish any of the jobs? In this story the reader senses the importance of the outcome long before the character does—and the outcome *is* important.

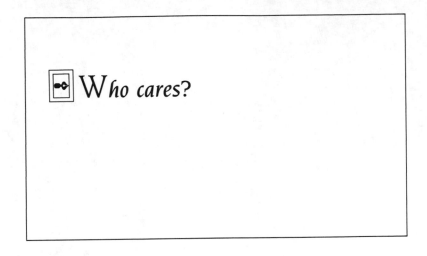

Who cares?

THE MORE YOU CARE ABOUT YOUR MAIN CHARACTER, THE more the reader will care.

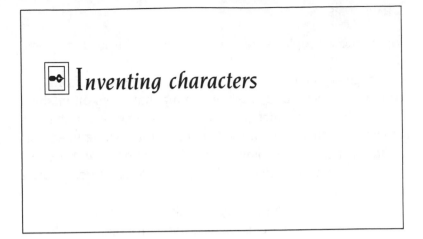

Inventing characters

BEFORE WE DISCUSS WAYS THAT WRITERS INVENT CHARACTERS we'll make a few general remarks. The main character is the core of storytelling. As you think about writing a story, and as you write it, concentrate on your main character. Concentrate on learning about and revealing her as deeply as you can.

Remember that stories are bred of people in conflict. People are more revealed in conflict than they are when everything goes along smoothly. There are often two kinds of conflict your main character will suffer: a long-standing conflict, bred perhaps of a flaw, and a specific conflict, which launches your story. For instance, a man who has been lazy for a long time is about to be fired from his job. Or a woman who has been competitive with her roommate for grades and in sports discovers the roommate is going out with her boyfriend. The long-term conflicts here are the laziness of the man and the competition between the roommates. The immediate conflicts that are essential for story-writing and that drive the stories forward are the threat of losing a job and the threat of losing a boyfriend.

We have heard several writers tell students, "Take me where I cannot go alone." This is wonderful advice. Tell the reader secrets about your main character's deepest yearnings, frustrations, dreams, and fears. Tell the reader things that are gossipy, too, because gossip reveals. Tell things about your main character that your reader could never know, even were she, in real life, the best friend of your character. In fiction we often know people more deeply than we do our family and friends.

Imagined characters in fiction often spring from the writer's character and experience. Our characters often share our traits and conflicts, our ways of seeing and behaving. Sometimes these similarities are conscious, sometimes not.

In our fiction, we combine parts of ourselves with people we know or have noticed or imagined. We create composite characters.

A good way to start a story is to think of a character with a flaw you possess that has caused you trouble—say, losing your temper. You might exaggerate that temper. Then you might think of a woman you know who usually controls her temper better than you, but when she does explode, throws things around; one time, she threw a book at a roommate. You might want to work with this explosive quality. Perhaps last week on the subway, you sat next to a woman with a plaid scarf and a mole under her chin and for some reason this has stuck in your mind; suddenly your character is wearing that scarf but the mole is now a blackhead, then many blackheads. You had a roommate once who used to drink too much, and again, somehow, the drinking and the woman with the scarf have become part of your character with the explosive temper. You're building a composite character. You're playing "what if," fooling around, imagining. The character has grown way beyond you now—she'll likely be in worse trouble than you've been, so you're free to say things about her you'd never say about yourself. And you've got a chance to understand things about her you probably don't understand about yourself.

Just as we advise you to write about places and worlds you know, we urge you to consider writing your first few stories about some part or parts of yourself that trouble you, that cause or have caused you conflict. And the reason here is the same: it's hard to learn to write stories, so start with material that's familiar; this will allow you to use convincing details and to draw on a character's deepest feelings. If a world and a character are unfamiliar to you, you're apt to use ordinary rather than distinctive details and to stay on the surface rather than to reveal your main character deeply.

Some new writers are reluctant to expose parts of themselves that embarrass them. But we've all suffered blows; we all are flawed. Surely each of us at least once, perhaps many times in our lives, has acted stupidly, selfishly, meanly, clumsily. Many people, as children anyway, and perhaps as adults, have lied, cheated, stolen, or failed at something. Some people are obsessive, others careless. Some procrastinate. Some are awed by the glamour of money, others resent rich people. Some are gloomy or manic or fearful or have panic attacks. Some people are bossy, some are passive. Some are rejected, others reject.

Remember, you aren't unique in your flaws. Some of us have overcome a flaw and can imagine what it would be like if we hadn't. Maybe we know someone with a blatant flaw that makes us nervous, because to a lesser extent we suffer it too. All this is potentially rich material for fiction. Writers dive into these problem areas and have the daring and imagination to project what they have discovered onto characters, distorting, exaggerating, inventing. Learn to do this. Go for the best, the deepest stories. Go for the jugular.

Think of someone whom you can't shake from your mind and who causes conflict for you—someone you're jealous of, someone who has been unfaithful to you, someone you love and hate. This person may be a wonderful character to write about. You can use him as a main character, or perhaps even better, write the story of the conflict from your point of view, from the view of someone having to cope with his jealousy or infidelity or confusion. Again, fool around with distortions, playing "what if," and build a composite character.

Another way to bring a character to life is to remember interesting people you've known. You might want to keep notes in a journal about what people say, do, fear, love; things they wear and own; things they seem to see clearly and not see clearly. Record their dreams and dreads and frustrations. Then, gradually, move into new territory—explore those things you have no way of knowing in a real person, but have always suspected or wondered about. Write these down. One insight will lead to another. Once you've established several traits in your character, you can let your imagination take over, discover what the character will or will not do, discover what the character wants and needs. You can probe and speculate and develop.

Pay attention to the small things about people you meet that reverberate for you: the woman last night who sat beside you at the movies and who smelled of garlic and cheese, the man who softly whistles "Dixie" again and again while he studies in the library during exam week, your neighbor who gardens in the rain. Often a small detail will trigger an idea for a character.

You'll hear writers talk about round and flat characters. Round characters are rich and complex; they have more than one side to them. You and your readers will get to know them deeply. Flat characters are one-dimensional. Your main character in a short story will be round. Because a story is so short and you haven't space to develop each person, your minor characters will be less round, most likely flat. But you can make characters memorable even if they appear only for a few lines, and you can bring them to life with some outstanding details. We discuss how to do this in the guide "Use Distinctive Details" on page 105, where Anne Whitney Pierce in "Sans Homme" shows a minor character, Mrs. Biondi, as being deaf and suffering from bursitis in her feet; we learn the old woman made anise tea and sugar cookies and was in love with one of the doctors on "General Hospital" on TV. These unusual details, carefully chosen, make Mrs. Biondi, alive, distinctive, and interesting. You'll use distinctive details with all your characters, but with the main character, you'll work to see what these details reveal, on a deep level, about him or her. You'll be showing how a main character, who may be infuriated by her mother, will a little later feel love for her, still later, rage, and then perhaps pity. In life we are not all one thing; we're often inconsistent in feeling and behavior. We need to get this complexity on our pages.

Exercises

1. Ethan Canin begins his story "Emperor of the Air" like this: "Let me tell you who I am. I am sixty-nine years old, live in the same house I was raised in, and have been a high school biology and astronomy teacher in this town so long that I have taught the grandson of one of my former students."

This is a wonderful way for a writer and for readers to learn about character. Invent a character and open with the Canin line, "Let me tell you who I am." Then let your character speak for herself. Not only will you discover information about her and her world, but you'll get that information in the character's own voice—and the voice, the way she says what she says, will reveal more than any list of facts ever could. Try this for at least a page. Once you get going, you may find yourself writing more: some characters get talking and it's hard to shut them up.

A note here: your character may not want to say, "Let me tell you who I am." She may say, "So you want the scoop on me, huh?" or, "Oh well, all right, I guess I'll try to tell you a few little things about myself if you're really interested, though I don't know why anyone would be."

2. Write in your journal the details of your main character's life. List what you know: age, height, objects on and in her bureau, education, scars, magazines she subscribes to, favorite music, TV shows, books, vacations spots, sports. How is her room furnished? What's in her closet, on the walls, and in the bedside table drawer? What are her habits, quirks, secrets, fears, and desires? Who are her friends and enemies? Can you work your way into her deepest yearnings, needs, dreams, and frustrations?

Be specific. Go beyond, "She likes to wear comfortable shoes," to her liking only flat leather shoes, lace up, brown with black laces. Rockport or Bass. Shoes made in Maine. She'll drive seven hours to Maine just to buy these shoes at outlet stores. She wears them with thick 100% cotton socks she orders from a gardening catalogue.

Then start writing about your character's conflict, how she regards the conflict, her greatest fears about that conflict, the worst and the best possible things she feels could result from the conflict. Now you're exploring how your character sees her world and reacts to it. What does your character do about the conflict? Write and discover what happens.

Many of your journal notes will never show up in your story. But your inner critic has eased off, you're writing freely, you're learning. Best of all, one good detail can lead to another which can lead to insight. You may even discover some good lines and passages that lead you into the story itself.

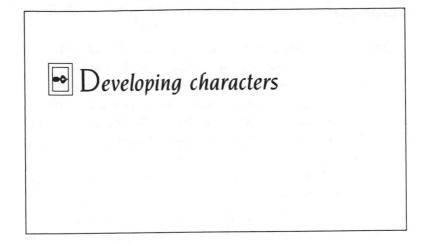

Developing characters

LET YOUR CHARACTERS TAKE OFF AND DO, THINK, SEE, AND SAY things that surprise you. Don't tie them up and push them around to fit a plot or idea you thought of before you began to write, or they'll be stiff and unbelievable. You will know some things about your main character before you write, but don't know too much or your story will be flat. Write to discover.

Once you have the kernel of a character in your mind or on the page, that character will develop as you write. Especially if the character experiences a specific conflict—for instance, the character with an uncontrollable temper has a *long-term* conflict with that temper. But the *specific, immediate* conflict of the story is that this time his girlfriend sees him hit someone, and she's so disgusted that she says she won't go out with him anymore. That's his specific conflict in the story. When you work with this kind of specificity, your job is easier.

If you don't know what the conflict is because you don't yet know your character well enough, you may want to write in your journal. Or you may write early drafts in which you get to know your character in his situation better. Sometimes writers think they're writing a story when they're really writing about characters. These are character sketches. Writers need to know the facts: Where do the characters live? What are they like? How do they act towards one another? What are their problems? What's unusual about them? Why do they do what they do? As writers write down these facts, and speculate, they often find stories.

Some writers suggest writing a day-in-the-life of a character: What time does she get up? What does she eat for breakfast? How does she take her coffee? By writing a detailed account, you may discover a story. When does this day turn sour for your character? Where is the conflict in her life? You are looking for this conflict. Once established, you'll know a lot more about where the story needs to go.

Much writing is practice writing. Some writers practice mostly in their heads, others on the page. It often takes a lot of warm-up writing and many revisions to develop a character, to see deeply into her. Writing fiction is a messy, non-linear process. Every night isn't concert night for a pianist either; every artist's sketch is not a masterpiece.

Character development is a process of getting to know your characters deeply. You'll learn as you write and revise, and revise again. Best of all, your characters will begin to say and do things that surprise you. They'll take on a life of their own.

We know people in stories in many ways: by what they do, say, feel, and think, and by the way others treat them. Main characters are also revealed by what they see, hear, smell, touch and taste, and how they regard all that they sense.

Some writers, like Flannery O'Connor in "Everything That Rises Must Converge," will step into a story and comment on characters, revealing things a character might never know about himself. Some writers, like Joan Didion and Ann Beattie, tend to rely more on external observations rather than going into their characters' heads at length or commenting often. Still others, like Andre Dubus, William Faulkner, Toni Morrison and Virginia Woolf, have their characters thinking, sometimes for long passages, about their deepest yearnings and frustrations.

To see how fully and profoundly we can know a character in a short story, read Faulkner's story, "Wash." The main character, Wash, is despised and called "poor white trash." He lives in the South in a shack on a run-down plantation owned by Colonel Sutpen. Wash longs to have a feeling of worth. And so, in order to stand his life, Wash takes the slight relationship he has with Sutpen and builds this up in his mind to something more significant than it is. The readers know Sutpen is weak and an alcoholic, but Wash also twists facts and evidence around in his head so that somehow he sees Sutpen as noble, strong, and brave. We understand that Wash must create these distortions in order to live: he must believe that he has a bond of sorts to a man who is noble and who will protect him and his family.

When it turns out that Sutpen won't look after Wash's granddaughter Milly (whom Sutpen impregnated), Wash's illusions come crashing down. He ends up killing Sutpen, killing his granddaughter and her baby, and setting fire to the building. In the final scene, we know that he will be killed.

How fascinating it is to see the specific ways that Wash distorts reality, to see the machinery of his mind at work. Study the long flashback that comes early in the story (right after the first space break) after readers have learned that Sutpen has no intention of caring for Wash's granddaughter, Milly. By the end of the story, you'll understand why Wash was driven to violence. And you'll learn new ways of probing your main characters' minds.

Reading a story as rich as "Wash" can discourage some new writers, but remember that Faulkner very likely didn't know a lot about Wash when he started writing. He set this man in a conflict and then wrote and discovered as he wrote. That's how writing works. One insight can lead to another and another, and these accumulate and can lead to wisdom.

Some writers fear they'll try to reveal a character deeply and fail. Don't worry if in the first few tries you say obvious or silly things. Everyone says or writes foolish things. Luckily we can revise. And what if you do revise many times and the insights are still obvious and superficial? This doesn't necessarily mean *you* are shallow; rather it might mean that at this time in your life with this particular story, you weren't able to see as profoundly as you wanted. You'll have other chances. But be willing to try to take that risk. Often.

There are many ways to get into characters' heads. As you write, don't forget to include what your character *sees* and how he thinks and feels about what he sees. This is a wonderful way for you the writer (and for the reader) to get to know your character. What a person notices or doesn't notice reveals him.

Consider including your character's fantasies. You can use expressions such as, "He wished he could . . ." or "She imagined (or pretended) she was. . . ." Lines as straightforward as these can extend a moment and reveal quite a lot about someone. Is his wish violent, erotic, child-like, noble? Characters' fantasies and dreams reveal dimensions beyond what they know and do.

Consider including your characters' deepest fears and hopes and desires. It's important to know what they want, because this is what drives them and is often a source of conflict.

People often feel one way one minute, another the next. We're inconsistent, ambivalent in our thoughts and actions, and this can enrich fiction. Again, check Flannery O'Connor's story "Everything that Rises Must Converge" to see how Julian longs to be free of his mother, yet is bound to her, tries to ignore her, then fights with her. A character may look at a boyfriend and want to hug him, then a moment later, want to slap him. Use such tension in your own writing.

Go as deeply as you can into your character as soon as you can. Don't hoard that one insight for the final revelation. Chances are if you know the insight before you write, it isn't terribly deep. It is through the act of writing and mulling over a character that we achieve depth. So put down everything you know about your character early in the story. One insight will lead to another and to another, and soon, your character will start informing and surprising you.

It's hard sometimes to tell everything at first. You're likely to fear there'll be no insights left after your initial purge, but try this method. It works.

Exercises

1. Think of trouble you've been in. One bad situation. What in your personality may have contributed to this trouble? Exaggerate that trait, and play with the situation so that it's more

dramatic now than it was, more critically important in your life. Start writing at the height of the conflict. You can always use a flashback later to fill in essential information.

2. Invent a character with an extreme way of seeing, of thinking; for instance, a woman who is paranoid, a man who is spoiled and who gets furious when anyone expects him to shape up, someone who is relentlessly gloomy or stupidly optimistic, someone who is very passive, or aggressive, stupid, mean, rigid, narcissistic, moralistic, compulsive, or panicky. Place this person in a situation where she or he is in trouble because of this way of seeing or thinking. There will be two conflicts here: the long-term one caused by the character's habit of seeing, and the immediate conflict precipitated by the character's flaw.

3. Read several stories and study the different ways writers reveal their main characters. Do the writers comment on their characters? Are there passages where the main characters think and feel and react? Are these long or short passages? Do you prefer stories where the writer reveals at length the thoughts and thinking processes of a main character or do you like stories where the writer renders the surface details and trusts that these will lead to deeper reverberations?

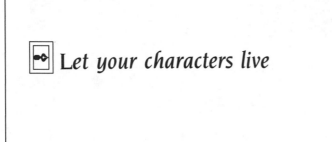

Let your characters live

PEOPLE DIE IN REAL LIFE AND THEY SOMETIMES DIE IN stories. Be careful though that you don't kill off characters for your own convenience: "And then they all died. The end." Make sure readers are prepared for the death; make sure the death is integral, not tacked on; make sure readers care enough about the character for the death to matter.

Your readers are alive—they tend to identify with living characters, and characters who go on living after the story concludes. Make sure your characters are alive on the page before you kill them off. A story dramatizes a conflict in a character's life—a critical time, a turning point, which implies what came before and what will come after.

Let your characters live.

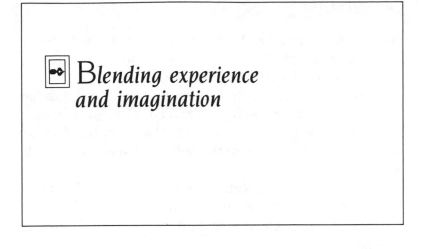

Blending experience and imagination

IS IT CHEATING TO TELL THE TRUTH? THAT IS, CAN FICTION BE fact? Can a story be true and still be considered fiction? How heavily can a fiction writer call on experience and still be called a fiction writer?

Who's to know? After you've written something from your life, distorted, extended it, you'll likely be unsure how much of the story did actually occur and how much was invention.

Fiction is a highly internal form. The external facts—what actually happened—are not usually as important as a character's perception of what happened. And who can agree on what happened? You and your sister remember quite differently the fight in which you tried to strangle her and stopped yourself at the last minute. Your mother may remember the incident as one in a series of annoying squabbles. Your father says the two of you got along beautifully your entire childhoods. Each person has a different point of view.

If your story is based not on direct experience but on something that has been told to you or something you read about, your treatment of the story can't help but change it considerably, perhaps beyond recognition. You will tell *your* truth—not the objective truth (whatever that is).

If you find yourself apologizing even to yourself—my fiction isn't really fiction, it's autobiography—stop it. Of course fiction is autobiography. Even a character who may appear to be your opposite has something of you in her. In fact the more different a character is from you, the more important it is to find commonality, something deep inside that you share—a fear or love of something, a secret, a compulsion, a frustration, a delusion, a belief, or a passion.

On the other hand, even a character who may appear to have much in common with you should be distinguished from you so that you can gain objectivity. Make him tall if you're short, make him younger or the father of twins. Distinguish. Separate.

All fiction connects with experience, even if the writer doesn't see the connection right away. The connection has to be there if the story is to have depth, if it is to arrive at some kind of truth.

The danger in writing too explicitly about an experience is that the experience might not be much of a story. We must embellish, reshape, find meaning.

Writers' lives usually have plenty of conflicts but few resolutions. We're not characters. In our stories, we create new patterns from scraps of experience and imagination. In developing characters, we explore minds and motives. We know our characters better than we know people around us because we get inside them. So even though a character may be based on someone we know or on ourselves, the more we write, the more we move away from the real to the imagined.

Exercises

1. Think of an experience you had that changed the way you saw yourself or someone else. Play with this on the page, perhaps sharpening the conflict, or shortening the time frame, maybe eliminating all but the two or three central characters. As you write, perhaps only jotting down notes, be playful and make many distortions, additions, subtractions. If a story comes of this, fine, but that's not the point. The point is to start from something that happened and let your imagination take over.

2. Describe yourself from the points of view of your best friend, your worst enemy, a parent, a teacher, or a boss.

You can see how truth is relative from this last exercise. Your enemy sees you very differently, we suspect, than you or your best friend do. Point of view is a marvelous distortion. In life, you see the world from the point of view of the egocentric "I." In fiction, you try on many points of view. You see through the eyes of your characters. Reality shifts. Truth reshapes itself.

We want to encourage you to use your imagination. When you're first learning to write stories, though, write stories that use your imagination to extend and distort experiences and feelings and worlds you know. Write about more exotic worlds in your journal. Later, when you know the tricks of the fiction trade better, branch out and explore characters and situations that are further removed from your world.

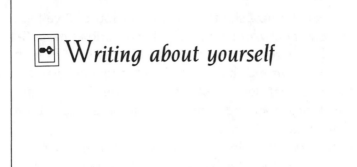

Writing about yourself

LIKE MANY WRITERS, YOU MAY BE HARSHER ON YOURSELF than on others when you fictionalize one of your experiences. Just because you dislike or are ashamed of one of your character traits, or of something you did, or of something that happened to you, don't let your main character come across as a one-dimensional fool, or as relentlessly mean or passive or goofy. Try to love your character as you write: have compassion for those flaws that get him in trouble, that cause him and other people pain. Be large-spirited and forgiving. You'll write with greater depth and insight if you're fair to your character than if you sneer.

Beware also of a need you may have to show your character as right, justified, or clever. Again, be fair.

Don't be afraid to write about yourself, whatever form you may take on the page. When our main characters have many of our personality traits and flaws, and the experiences they go through are like ones that happened to us, we tend to cringe when the characters say or think or do things that reveal them in unflattering lights. We hate to have these characters fail or be defeated. We feel exposed, embarrassed, threatened. Don't undermine your story because you need to have your main character triumph or be honorable or safe. Remember: this is fiction. You're extending, exaggerating, lying. Tell yourself: This is not I. This is she.

To gain objectivity on yourself as you write, create someone who is physically different from you. Know in detail how that person looks and how she feels about her looks. Give her a flaw, strength, hobby, or mannerism that you don't have. Get one or several of these going early in the story so they influence your prose. It may help to make your main character a little, but not a lot, less intelligent than you. This can give writers distance from and compassion for their poor bumbling characters.

Some writers clip a colored picture of a person from a magazine and paste it over their desks as a reminder: I'm writing about this person, up there, not just about me.

 # Exercise

Think of an experience where you behaved poorly—even better, an experience that causes you to cringe when you think of it. First, write very quickly about what happened and how you now feel about it. This will be an outpouring. Then create a character like you but with enough superficial changes so that you can write about her or him and the experience. For example, make her a little more naïve than you. Name her. We'll say her name is Astrid. Pretend that you are Astrid's best friend, a person who is wise and compassionate. Write in your journal about Astrid's experience.

Secrets

FICTION WRITERS HAVE NO SECRETS. ALL OUR FEELINGS AND thoughts—brilliant, mundane, and depraved—are revealed in our stories. In essays, our feelings and thoughts are revealed directly. In fiction, we attribute them to our characters; we explore and extend them.

Fiction is not an escape from our deepest feelings and dreams and fears and experiences, nor it is camouflage. It's an enormous magnifying glass. If you are a well-adjusted, happy person you'll have to dig deep for the trouble that is the fuel of fiction or be sensitive enough to learn it from others around you. On the other hand, if, like most writers (and perhaps most people, if they probed deeply) you are troubled by many things, flawed in a number of ways, difficult to live with, and riddled with nasty secrets, then you have an advantage.

Through fiction we reveal parts of ourselves that we'd never discuss with our best friends, that we could not possibly articulate except through fiction. Writers reveal all their secrets, eventually, so don't try to make your characters out as noble if you know little about nobility. Flaubert said about his tragically flawed character, Madame Bovary, "C'est moi." He was saying that *he* was Madame Bovary.

Don't waste time, energy, and paper evading your secrets, trying to protect yourself. Everyone you know has flaws, secrets. That's why people love to read about flawed characters. Accept that the greatest writers in the world have flaws, too, perhaps more than most people, and they often work with these in their fiction. It takes courage. Good writers have courage.

◖ Exercise

List your secrets. You will not show this list to anyone. List experiences you don't want anyone to know about. List fears. List desires and dreams and yearnings. List frustrations. List thoughts you're ashamed of. List socially, emotionally and/or politically incorrect deviant leanings and actions. List your enemies. List people you have failed in some way or who have failed you. List your lovers, real or imagined. Recall your deepest shame, your greatest mistakes and failures, the worst thing you ever did, your worst pain. List your worst preoccupation or obsession.

These secrets are at the heart of fiction, even when writers deny it, which many of us do to protect ourselves. These secrets influence our writing just because they're secrets. They've been building up inside us and need to get out. We often tell our friends about the good things in our lives and therefore we are aware of them. The bad things need to be worked out through our characters in stories.

Disguising people you know

SOME PEOPLE FEEL LIKE TRAITORS AS THEY WRITE ABOUT the flaws of friends or family. They worry to the point of writer's block that they'll hurt or anger someone, reveal a secret, betray a trust. There may be the worry of being sued should the story be printed.

If you make minor changes in the character and situation, most people won't recognize themselves. Or they'll say that yes, this is somewhat like me, but look here, the person in the story is a stutterer and loves to shop and that's not me at all. People don't want to see themselves as silly, cruel, stupid, or weak, and they will seize on superficial changes you've made to protect themselves.

If you're writing about someone you can't stand, you run the danger of making her one-dimensional unless you distance yourself. Be fair to your characters. No one will believe a character is all bad.

As with writing about yourself, there are practical ways to protect others and to protect your right to write honestly:

- Change the physical looks of the character.

- Give the character on the page a physical or emotional flaw or a strength the real person lacks—a limp, a lisp, a loud voice, a gloomy way of seeing the world, the ability to read a novel a night, to repair a motorcycle, or to play excellent chess or grow beautiful roses.

- Change the person's job, hobbies, taste in clothes, or food.

- Place events in another city or town or state that you know well.

- Think of something the real-life person hates and have the fictional character love it—fishing, sloppiness, science fiction, the color blue.

Get one or two of the distortions going fairly soon in your story so you're forced to work with them.

Beware of distorting to the point where you lose enthusiasm for writing about the character.

Some writers write what they need to in a first draft and later make changes to protect people they know.

Never show, never mention the story to the person you're writing about while the story's in process. This can kill the writing. In fact, don't show the story to that person at all. Most new writers don't send their early stories to magazines. Should you want to, and should your piece be accepted, months will elapse between acceptance and publication. You will have chances to make even more changes at the last minute. Probably you won't want to by then.

⊶ Exercise

If you can't stand a person you want to use as a character, and you fear he'll be one dimensional, write a letter that you'll tear up later telling that person everything you ever wanted to say. Have a temper tantrum on the page if you want. Then write your story and be fair.

⊡ Respect your sensibility, your vision, your temperament

WRITE THE STORIES ONLY YOU CAN WRITE. WRITE STORIES that interest you, not what you think you ought to be interested in. Write about people who fascinate you, not about people you think readers will want to read about. Trust your raw material, the worlds you know, your vision. Don't affect a sensibility, an attitude, a way of seeing and writing that's foreign to you or you'll be a pale imitation of someone else. Your favorite writers don't imitate others; that's one of the reasons you admire them.

A woman we know tried to write like Hemingway. She was in her forties and had children. She loved Hemingway's stories, as we do, but her characters carried around complicated backgrounds and pasts that haunted them. Her experiences, her temperament and ways of seeing her world were different than Hemingway's, an ex-patriot. She was helped much more by studying Flannery O'Connor, Toni Morrison, and William Faulkner, whose characters are often grounded in pasts or ways of seeing that are complex. Of course the writer was helped by Hemingway, too, but for a while she needed to study writers with visions closer to hers. From them she learned specific techniques that helped her explore the complexities of her characters' lives.

If you're the kind of person who feels close to her or his characters, identifies with them, respect this in yourself. If you see people with detachment, respect this, too.

Below are some very different sensibilities and voices at work:

"A new person, it was said, had appeared on the esplanade: a lady with a pet dog. Dmitry Dmitrich Gurov, who had spent a fortnight at Yalta and had got used to the place, had also begun to take an interest in new arrivals." (Anton Chekhov, "The Lady With the Pet Dog")

In Virginia Woolf's story, below, the main character, who has just walked into a party, goes to a mirror and looks at her new dress. Woolf writes: "No! It was not *right* . . . for oh these men, oh these women, all were thinking—'What's Mabel wearing? What a fright she looks! What a hideous new dress!'" (Virginia Woolf, "The New Dress")

"Back in the days when everyone was old and stupid or young and foolish and me and Sugar were the only ones just right, this lady moved on our block with nappy hair and proper speech and no makeup." (Toni Cade Bambara, "The Lesson")

"For even his pride of family, his love for the place of his birth, were confused and paradoxical.
    Proud of his father, his name, and the names of kin. His hive of kinfolk in Devon. Yet also ashamed; for why were they now left clinging to memories or dreaming of other futures? Proud and ashamed and ashamed of being so." (George Garrett, *Death of the Fox*)

"The Grandmother didn't want to go to Florida. She wanted to visit some of her connections in east Tennessee and she was seizing at every chance to change Bailey's mind. Bailey was the son she lived with, her only boy." (Flannery O'Connor, "A Good Man Is Hard To Find")

"Kugelmass, a professor of humanities at City College, was unhappily married for the second time. Daphne Kugelmass was an oaf. He also had two dull sons by his first wife, Flo, and was up to his neck in alimony and child support." (Woody Allen, "The Kugelmass Episode")

"Murphy's drunk on the bright verge of still another Christmas and a car door slams. Then he's out in the headlights and in bed waking up the next afternoon with Annie kissing his crucified right fist." (Mark Costello, "Murphy's Xmas")

And finally, this piece which is the beginning of a novel: "I was eleven when the new doctor came to Sumner County. Prettiest man I ever saw. Came around to the school, looked at everybody in the class. When he got to me, he said, 'You're mighty tall to be in just the sixth grade.' I hunched over and made an S out of my backbone." (Margaret-Love Denman, A *Scrambling After Circumstance*)

Even in short quotations like these, the voices of these writers are distinct.

In our guide, "Suggested Readings," we include lists of books by writers who have different approaches to fiction, different ways of seeing, different sensibilities and voices. This guide may help you find writers with visions somewhat similar to yours.

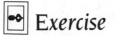 # Exercise

To see and hear different writers' voices, read out loud the first page of ten stories in an anthology, one right after another. Say to yourself that all these writers wrote about what they knew, trusted their ways of seeing, their characters' experiences. Tell yourself that you will do this, too.

PLOT

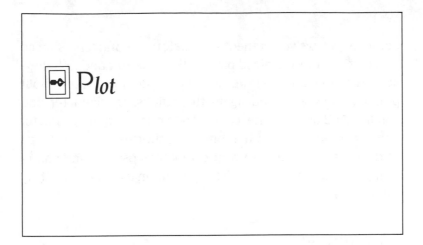

Plot

WE RARELY MENTION PLOT IN OUR CLASSES. INSTEAD WE discuss character and conflict, because when writers concentrate on their main characters who are in conflict and when they write to discover insights into their psyches, plot will evolve. A character's reactions to her mounting conflict will cause something to happen.

In our guide, "What Is a Story," we discuss the need for stories to have a beginning, a middle, and an end. In stories, a change occurs. As a result of this change, life is never exactly the same anymore. The main character and/or the reader may gain a new insight. A new light may be shed on a situation or person. Sometimes the change is more dramatic; for instance, someone may die or a couple separate.

Plot is the pattern created within the story, the accumulation of information in a careful sequence to build tension, to build a crisis that will explode, to allow for a satisfying resolution. Plot is much more than what happens in a story. It is the way in which events are connected, and, in a sense, it is the pattern of revelation.

The difference between a story and a character sketch may well be this pattern of revelation. The same information in one order is simply an accumulation of fine detail about a character; in another order, that information has the tension, forward motion, and drama of a story.

New writers sometimes fall into the trap of thinking up plots before they write their stories, but this is a mistake because, as we've warned you before, characters shoved around to fit preconceived plots will be shallow and unbelievable. We advise you as we do our students to forget about plot. Go back and read again the guides on character and conflict. And as you write, concentrate on your main character and her world, focus on her long- and short-term conflicts, go as deeply as you can into your character's psyche, and something will happen. The conflict will erupt in a crisis. Your story will have a plot.

Exercise

If nothing is happening in one of your stories, read three of your favorite published stories to see what happens in them. Notice how the conflict mounts and erupts in a crisis and that then there is a tapering off, a denouement. Notice how the plot depends on character. Pay attention to how the main character responds to his conflict and how this determines the outcome of the story. Then summarize what happens in a few sentences.

DETAILS

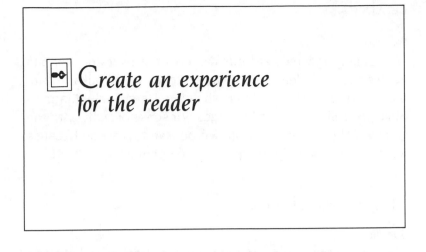

Create an experience for the reader

WE LOVE TO READ STORIES, TO STEP INTO OTHER WORLDS and see the worlds as the main characters see and feel them. We long to live other lives, to be transported. A good story, rather than analyzing an event, creates an experience for the reader. That's one of the reasons we read.

To create a world that your reader can believe in and can step into, use the language of fiction. It is sensuous, full of details, facts, and information. Rely on the five senses. Readers must see, hear, touch, taste, and smell. *Most important: Readers must see.* A reader who can't see is not included and won't experience what is happening on the page.

Another way to talk about the importance of using details is to say "Show don't tell." Writers are urged to reveal what happens, not summarize it. (Sometimes artful telling is necessary and adds to the story. For now, however, we want to stress the importance of showing, because it's a skill writers need to practice.) Be specific. Avoid vague, general statements in your stories. Below, we give examples of vague prose that tells, and specific prose that shows.

Vague:
"It was a beautiful serene spot." That's telling. It's summarizing. Readers can't see, hear, touch, taste, or smell anything when they read such a vague sentence.

Specific:

"The small brown water birds came to the river and hopped across the mud, leaving brown scratches in the alkali-white moss and fern leaves." This is showing. Here, Leslie Marmon Silko, in "Yellow Woman," engages our sense of sight with the sensuous language of fiction. We believe this scene because we see it; we participate in what's happening.

Vague:

"They sat rather idly outside."

Specific:

"She sat on the rattan chaise in the hot October twilight and watched BZ throw the ice cubes from his drink one by one into the swimming pool." Joan Didion, *Play It As It Lays*.

Vague:

"It is very hot."

Specific:

"It is a hundred degrees outside, and bright white. Each time someone goes in or out of the co-op a gust of air conditioning flies out of the automatic doors, raising dust from the cement." David Leavitt, "Territory."

Vague:

"She was extremely frugal."

Specific:

"Being of a thrifty nature, she ate slowly, picking up from the table the crumbs from her loaf of bread—a twelve pound loaf which was baked specially for her and lasted twenty days." Gustave Flaubert, "A Simple Heart."

Here is a passage from John Yount's novel, *Trapper's Last Shot*. In it, a boy jumps into a swimming hole and finds it is full of snakes—cottonmouth moccasins. Try to imagine writing this scene. Some writers might be tempted to use words like terror, horror, frightful, disgusting. Yount shows us the things that produced the terror—that is, he writes with details, specifics. Later in this passage he shows us the reactions of townspeople to the boy's death, and again, he's specific.

The next day five boys started out to go swimming in the south fork of the Harpeth river. Except for a thin crust like pastry shell over the pink dust, there was no evidence of the rain. As they walked toward the river, the heat droned and shimmered in the fields, and locusts sprang up before them to chitter away and drop down and then spring up again as they came on. When they got among the trees on the river bank, the oldest of them, who was fourteen, shucked quickly out of his britches and ran down the bank and out on a low sycamore limb and, without breaking stride, tucked up his legs and did a cannonball into the water. The surface all around, even to the farthest edge, roiled when he hit as if the pool were alive, but they didn't see the snakes at first. The boy's face was white as bleached bone when he came up. "God," he said to them, "don't come in!" And though it was no more than a whisper, they all heard. He seemed to struggle and wallow and make pitifully small headway though he was a strong swimmer. When he got in waist deep water, they could see the snakes hanging on him, dozens of them, biting and holding on. He was already staggering and crying in a thin, wheezy voice and he brushed and slapped at the snakes trying to knock them off. He got almost to the bank before he fell, and though they wanted to help him, they couldn't keep from backing away. But he didn't need them then. He tried only a little while to get up before the movement of his arms and legs lost purpose, and he began to shudder and then to stiffen and settle out. One moccasin, pinned under his chest, struck his cheek again and again, but they could see he didn't know it for there was only the unresponsive bounce of flesh.

According to the coroner who saw the body, the boy had been bitten close to two hundred times.

Sheriff Tate Newcome and Deputy Earl Wagner dynamited the swimming hole that same afternoon and reported that just beneath the surface, there were hundreds, perhaps thousands of cottonmouth moccasins, the bodies of which practically formed a dam at the lower end of the hole and all but stopped the flow of water.

For days afterwards no one could think or talk of anything else. Some said they had heard of snakes congregating like that before, but nobody seemed to know what caused it. The drought, some offered. A biology professor at the college in

Seneca was quoted in the paper as saying that it might have been a kind of breeding orgy that belonged, evolutionarily speaking, to a more primitive time. Some thought it was more than likely a consequence of the infernal testing of atomic bombs. And some felt very strongly that it was a judgement on them, connected somehow with the disrespect of the young for the old, the Communists taking over, the niggers getting too big for their britches—a sure sign given them to show the degeneration and sinful nature of the times.

But whatever their disagreement about its cause, everybody in Cocke County had heard what had happened, and they couldn't free their minds of the thought of it, nor their stomachs of a sick and shaky feeling that lasted for days and days. Even Deputy Earl Wagner—who, given any back talk, could come out of his hip pocket with a sap and beat a man almost to death and all the time be sucking his teeth as if he were bored—when he told about setting off the dynamite, would blink and swallow and rest the heel of his hand on the butt of his holstered pistol for comfort. "They was snakes all over the whole Goddamned river," he'd say, "blowed out on the bank and clean up in the trees, and that hole there, where that boy jumped in, after we taken and set off that dynamite, was solid snake bellies. Look like a bowl of spaghetti." The men standing about to listen in Sharaw, standing by the barbershop or in front of the courthouse, shook their heads when he told it and grunted as if they had been poked with a stick. And after, they seemed unable to walk away and looked at the ground or off at the horizon, their eyes glazed over with thought.

Try this. Summarize the first paragraph in a general way, and then read it as Yount wrote it. Do this all through, and you'll appreciate the power of his prose even more. For instance, Yount could have written, "Even the deputy was deeply affected." That would have been vague. Instead, Yount names the Deputy—Earl Wagner—and gives us a specific example of how tough he is: He " . . . could come out of his hip pocket with a sap and beat a man almost to death and all the time be sucking his teeth as if he were bored." We also hear what Wagner says about the snakes and we see the men, not on an empty stage, but standing by the barbershop or in front of the courthouse. We're included, not given vague generalizations that leave us out.

Caroline Gordon says writers should try to use three of the five senses in important scenes. The sense of smell can bring readers into an experience fast. Some writers say we should refer to all five senses in an important scene.

Sometimes a writer may think she's shown more than she has, especially if the scene is placed in a location she knows well. Her mind fills in details that aren't on the page. You must look at what is on your pages, see as your readers see, and then decide if you've included sufficient detail.

How many details should you use? Some writers like Alice Munro, William Faulkner, Gloria Naylor, and Mark Helprin tend to use many details in their descriptions. Others like Raymond Carver and Joan Didion tend to use fewer, although those they do use are brilliantly chosen and make our imaginations fill in the gaps. You will find what works best for you. We do want to say this though: new writers are often stingy with details. Remember that it's easier to take them out than to put them in. At the same time we give you a warning from Chekhov: "If in the first chapter you say that a gun hung on the wall, in the second or third chapter it must without fail be discharged."

If you're overusing details, not knowing what to include, what to leave out, stop. Ask yourself: What is this story really about? What is important? What is the conflict? If a man bursts into your room and points a gun at you, will you notice whether his shoelaces are black or brown? No, because the main conflict has to do with whether or not he'll pull the trigger. You'll notice the hair on his index finger wrapped around the trigger, and you'll pay attention to his expression, trying to gauge what he'll do next. A clear conflict and knowing or at least sensing the story's theme will inform you about what details to include.

Develop the habit of being specific, of seeing the world as a writer does. When you walk downtown, notice the old man holding balloons on the street corner. He's drunk and his shirt is stained, but oddly he always wears pressed pants, and today they're shiny and yellow. If you watch this man enough and think about the details you notice, and what they mean, you'll learn about him. This holds true for writing about characters, too.

Exercises

1. Four times each day for the next week—whether you're at the beach, waiting for the pasta to boil, at a concert, or in a doctor's waiting room—stop whatever you're doing, pull out your notebook and write what you see, hear, smell, taste, touch. Writer and teacher Donald Graves calls these "writing occasions": taking a few minutes to record your life as it is happening.

2. Translate these abstract, generalized sentences into the language of fiction.
   a. The dog looked mean.
   b. She was paranoid.
   c. He tried everything he could to attract her attention.
   d. It was a depressing kind of day.
   e. She hated him.
   f. He was obsessive.
   g. The room was a terrible mess.

3. Find some abstract, generalized sentences in your fiction. Translate them into sensuous prose.

4. Take one of your favorite passages from a published short story. Rewrite it, using vague language. Read aloud the published piece, then what you rewrote, and finally, the published piece again. You'll see and hear the differences.

Some people think writers are vague types, oblivious to their surroundings, but they watch with wonderfully clear, accurate eyes.

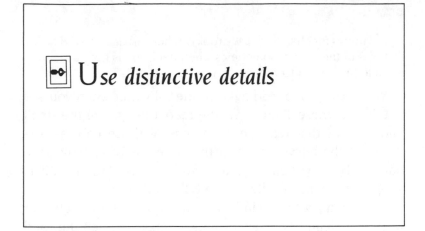

Use distinctive details

IF YOU INCLUDE A SHORT PARTY SCENE IN YOUR STORY, MAKE it unlike any other party in the world. Never say "typical" party, or "typical" anything. It's up to writers to see beyond, beneath, and through the stereotype. Each classroom, dog, old woman, pilot, river, potato, child, dentist's office, waiter, bus; each moment of love, fear, jealousy, joy, hate, anger, grief; each moment; each character—however briefly he or she appears— should be distinctive. Look for the revealing details that distinguish someone or something from every other person or thing. Look for necessary details. It is such a pleasure to read a story full of meaningful, memorable details; it is like slogging across the mud flat to read dull, predictable ones.

Don't say, "She was my babysitter who lived downstairs; we watched a lot of TV together." Instead, distinguish the sitter as does Anne Whitney Pierce in *The North American Review* story, "Sans Homme." Mrs. Biondi appears only in this paragraph, but she is unlike any other baby sitter in the world.

> Before Dusty came, those two hours after school before Lily got home I used to spend downstairs at Mrs. Biondi's apartment. She made me sugar cookies and anise tea. She was just about deaf and we watched the soaps together, but when her hearing aid was on the fritz, she'd shout, "What'd that nurse say?" and I'd shout back, "She said the baby was born without his thumb!" and then we'd cry together. We were both in love with the same doctor on "General Hospital," one whose fan mail was slipping, we read in the *TV Guide*, because he was growing bald and stout. In return for her kindness, Lily and I

did things for Mrs. Biondi. We took out her garbage and did her taxes in the spring. Sometimes when her bursitis got bad, she called me down to rub her feet.

You know you're reading a wonderful writer when you see details like these. Pierce gets the reader imagining the smell and heat of that tea, the sweetness of those cookies, the flicker of the television. Even the soaps are distinctive; the baby is born without a thumb and a doctor's fan mail is slipping because he's becoming bald and stout.

When you get these kinds of details going all through your work, you'll find yourself gaining energy, momentum, and enthusiasm as you write; you'll find your characters coming alive, informing you of what happens next.

Exercise

Stand or sit in a restaurant, train station, laundromat, or supermarket. Note the specific details that reveal several people and objects as unlike any other people and objects. For instance, the man with one walleye, the woman with unlaced work boots, the cashier whose voice rises and falls like a Mozart trill as she talks to customers, the roll of toilet paper someone left in the frozen orange juice section of the market. Do this exercise every day for twenty minutes a day for two weeks. The details in your lists and in your stories will improve.

Develop the habit of enjoying distinctive details as you go through life and as you read; slow down and savor them, and get them on your pages.

Use gossip

SOME NEW WRITERS WHO WANT TO WRITE ABOUT LARGE, important themes neglect details that seem to them insignificant, or worse, the preoccupation of small-minded gossips. And yet, by examining one detail or fact after another, writers arrive at larger truths. Don't take the elevator to your theme; don't write knowing the theme before you begin your story. If you do, your details and facts and characters will feel contrived. Instead, earn your way to meaning. Start with small pieces of information, seeing their significances as you go along, and write to discover what these details add up to.

In "Leaving the Yellow House," Saul Bellow tells us wonderfully gossipy things about his main character Hattie. She's vulnerable and needy. There's a limit to how long her neighbors at Sego Desert Lake can be counted on to help her out. She has tantrums when she plays canasta. She once went to Paris to study the organ, but now she doesn't "... know a note from a skillet." She keeps A-1 Sauce and ketchup and opened jars of fruit on the shelves of her library. Still, she's a lady, Bellow writes, and she has good silver and china and engraved stationery. Before she goes to town once a week to drink with her cronies at Marian Nabot's Silvermine Hotel and to buy groceries—"frozen meat pies and whiskey"—Hattie takes off her dirty aviator's jacket and puts on a girdle, a dress, and high-heeled shoes. After going to these efforts, she draws her lipstick in a straight line across her mouth, not following the V in her upper lip. These details could be viewed as petty—we can almost hear someone whisper, "Yesterday I went to Hattie's house, and there, on a shelf in her library, was A-1 Sauce!"—but as the details accumulate, we gain insights into Hattie's character. She fascinates us. As importantly, Bellow himself likely was delighted and surprised as he wrote these "gossipy" details down, and for every one he wrote, more probably came to him. An accumulation of good details can lead to wisdom. This is how writing works.

Stuff your stories with A-1 Sauce.

Gossip between characters can fascinate you and your readers. Jane tells Sung Ho that their roommate slips out of their apartment each morning between two and three and comes back in before five a.m. Where does he go? Why is it a secret? Perhaps during the next few days, Jane and Sung Ho report to each other on the roommate's whereabouts, become obsessed with clues and speculations. Suddenly we're as interested in the gossips as we are in knowing what the roommate is up to.

Community gossip can enter fiction. In "There's a Garden of Eden," Ellen Gilchrist begins her story with a group perspective on her main character: "Scores of men, including an exgovernor and the owner of a football team, consider Alisha Terrebone to be the most beautiful woman in the state of Louisiana." Then the narrator comments in a gossipy way: "If she is unhappy what hope is there for ordinary mortals? Yet here is Alisha, cold and bored and lonely, smoking in bed."

We learn on the first page of this story about Alisha's bed and her husband, who isn't fun anymore, and now has a bed of his own in another place. We learn she's had three husbands so far, we learn who they were, and we learn their respective financial statuses. We learn that now she spends a lot of time in bed reading, drinking coffee, and cutting photographs from magazines. These details reveal Alisha as a rich character, and we learn not only about her, but the people who talk about her.

In "Dry September," Faulkner tells us that there is a rumor going around the town, " . . . something about Miss Minnie Cooper and a negro." We have to read on. In this story the gossip leads to wisdom not only about Miss Minnie Cooper and the black man, but also about the community.

Some writers will write a whole story from the perspective of community opinion and gossip. They'll use the word "they" throughout. In other stories the perspective shifts between the community and the main character about whom people gossip. Still other stories start with a community's view and then focus on the main character, staying with that person until the end or until very near the end where, only briefly, the point of view returns to public opinion and judgment. In your early stories, we urge you to stay with one perspective because it's simpler.

If you write from the perspective of a gossip, remember that there is a reason one person becomes fascinated by another and needs to gossip. Readers should understand this need and see how the gossiper is affected by what he learns.

Exercises

1. Think of someone you know or knew about whom people gossiped; for example, a student we'll call Deno had an affair with his geography teacher in your high school. Start writing about the rumors, changing them or inventing new ones if you like. You may want to mention that Jake said that Deno had been seen at the beach with the teacher, then Cherise added that she'd heard another piece of information, but it seemed to you that . . . and so forth. Then as you record these facts and rumors, decide whether you want to keep telling the story from the perspective of several students, or from your perspective. Or you may decide to write from the perspective of Deno or the teacher.

2. Invent a character. Start with a sentence that includes a seemingly small detail or details that fascinate you. Then write another sentence with more details, facts, information about the character. Then another and so forth. What kind of character are you creating? What do these facts reveal?

3. Imagine that an aluminum suitcase has been left under some bushes in a public park. You come upon it. What's in it? What does this tell you about the owner? Or imagine you find a large purse on the street. What's in it?

4. Three people discover they've just won a seven-thousand-dollar one-week trip to Paris. They must pack and be at the airport in one hour. What will each person bring?

5. Two people—they don't know each other and live in separate parts of the city or town—have just learned that their spouses (or brothers or sisters or parents) have died. Decide who is dead and what the relationships are to the survivors. In the next hour, what does each person do? After you write, you may want to read Kate Chopin's "Story of an Hour," which is about a woman's reactions when she believes her husband has died.

Develop the habit of appreciating small details in your daily life, your reading, and your writing. And remember that the more rich, juicy details you include in your stories, the more fun you'll have writing, and the more you'll learn about your characters.

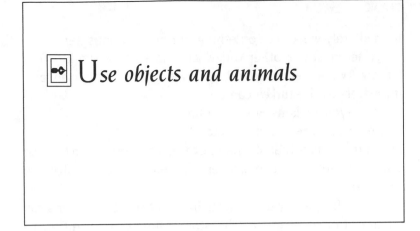

Use objects and animals

WHAT WE FEEL, THINK, AND DO ABOUT OBJECTS AND ANIMALS can reveal us. People develop attachments and aversions to things like moles on their chins, knives, guitars, peony bushes, a neighbor's barking dog, a roommate's smelly socks, pickles, worms, trains, a ring, a photograph, a shabby coat, a stylish hat, a spot on the wall. Be alert to those things your main character feels strongly about. Get these going on your pages. It will help you and your readers learn about your character.

In *Baron in the Trees* by Italo Calvino, the title character feels so much empathy for the snails in the barrel down cellar (snails to be eaten by the household) that he loosens the lid to set them free.

People project their feelings toward another person onto objects. If your main character loves her roommate, she'll likely think her hat with a blue jay feather and her pink cow coffee mug are charmingly eccentric. If your main character dislikes her roommate, she'll hate the stupid hat and think the mug is just like the roommate: tacky.

Objects can lead writers and readers into stories. They can suggest conflicts. In some cases, they embody conflicts. In "The Turkey Season," Alice Munro's main character, a girl of fourteen, works on a farm gutting turkeys. Her character is revealed as she thinks about the turkey carcasses while in bed. She closes her eyes and sees the bloody carcasses hanging upside down, but they do not revolt her as they might many people. She views them as a job she will do, and immediately we know something important about her.

We learn about other turkey gutters as they work in the factory. Two sisters, Lily and Marjorie, talk ". . . abusively and intimately to the turkey carcasses.

'Don't you nick me, you old bugger!'

'Aren't you the old crap factory!'"

The narrator says that she had never heard women who spoke that way. Here the two women as well as the narrator are revealed.

Writers frequently use objects in their titles and never stray far from those objects as the stories unfold. In addition to Alice Munro's "The Turkey Season," you also might want to read Cynthia Ozick's "The Shawl," Ernest Hemingway's "Cat in the Rain," and William Faulkner's "The Brooch." At the heart of Ann Beattie's "Janus" is a lucky bowl that the main character, a real estate agent, places strategically in the homes she is trying to sell as she presents the homes to buyers. Later in the story we learn the bowl was a gift from a past lover, and its significance increases.

These stories may give you an idea for a story. But even if they don't, be aware that your characters can be revealed by their reactions to things they feel strongly about.

◄═► Exercises

1. Think of an object that you or your main character or someone you know loves or hates, or best of all, feels conflicted about. Describe the object in detail through the eyes of your main character. Be playful and make connections between the object and why it's important to your character, perhaps writing about how the character came to own it, or how the character's attitude towards it has changed. Show the character in contact with the object. See what happens.

2. Invent two characters, neighbors, who live near a man with a dog that barks and often trespasses on their property. What will each neighbor think and do and say about the dog?

Maybe one of these exercises gave you an idea for a story. If not, you've practiced descriptive writing and probing the mind of a character. You've been playful—seen how far you can loop out from the original object, seen how many connections presented themselves to you. You have been particular. You're getting into good habits—paying attention to the small things your characters notice.

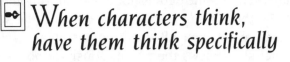

When characters think, have them think specifically

IN LIFE IF A WRITER THINKS OF WHETHER SHE WANTS TO SPEND a weekend at a cabin in Maine by herself or to go to Boston to see friends and some plays, she might decide that she's had a busy year and she needs solitude. She'll go to the cabin. But behind these general thoughts are specific facts and details on which she bases her decision: She's been writing, teaching, being with family and friends for a semester; her cousin has spent a month with her. And she loves that cabin. It is what she knows about the cabin that convinces her to go there. The nearest neighbors to the north are a whole national forest away, to the south, about twenty miles, and to the east and west, about eight miles. Her son built the cabin. She loves the way it sits high on a hill a mile away from the road, loves the potbellied wood stove, the big round windows on the south wall overlooking the Moriah Mountain Range. There is no telephone, no electricity. She will park just off the road and back pack up an old logging road, stopping at Resolute Brook where she'll rest for a while on that boulder shaped like Africa. Then she'll pick a few Lemon daylilies she planted last fall, and when she gets to the cabin, she'll put them in the pale green vase her mother gave her. After this, if it looks as though the evening will be cool, she'll put logs in the stove and get a fire going.

As the writer makes her decision in life, she won't think consciously of each of those details, but if a story involved this decision, some of the details would be included so readers would know why she chose the cabin. Probably the writer would describe some details about her life at home and at work, too. If the visiting cousin were difficult, the writer would be exact about him. All these details *are* part of her choice whether she reviews them consciously or not. Again, remember there is a difference between life and art.

When your characters think on your pages, especially when they think for a long time, be sure readers can see the place where the characters sit or stand or walk as they think. Place influences us. It's part of context, and it counts.

We have discussed James Joyce's story "Eveline" previously as a decision story. It is also an excellent example of an author grounding the thinking of his main character in a specific setting with exact details.

Before Joyce shows us what Eveline is thinking, he tells us details like this: she is sitting by a window, her head leans against the window curtains and she smells " . . . the odour of dusty cretonne." Joyce establishes that smell of cretonne early and it seems to pervade the entire scene. From the window, Eveline sees few people. Then a man passes by and Joyce is so specific about his footsteps that we're prepared to believe everything he writes: " . . . she heard his footsteps clacking along the concrete pavement and afterwards crunching on the cinder path before the new red houses." Readers hear the clacking along concrete and then the crunching on the cinder path. We see, smell, and hear. We're given three of the five senses, and they pull us deeply into the story. Now we're ready to get into Eveline's mind for several pages.

Eveline recalls her brothers and sisters and her growing up in this neighborhood. She would probably, in life, picture in her mind the children she played with rather than naming them, but this is a story. Joyce names the children from several families including a boy called Keogh, who is a cripple. Little Keogh calls out when he sees Eveline's father come with his blackthorn stick. These are precise details. Later, Eveline thinks about her father, who frightens her. Again, in life she would probably experience a vague fear as she thought of him. But that fear is based on experience, and Joyce wisely records some specific information that includes the reader in why Eveline was afraid. We learn the father drank too much, fought her for money on Saturday nights when she brought home her weekly wages of seven shillings. Money counts. Joyce tells us what she earns. The father would squander his money, but usually Eveline could get some from him and she'd rush off to market " ... holding her black leather purse tightly in her hand" as she went to the stores. Eveline would never in life think, "I take the money and hold my black leather purse tightly in my hand." That's the art of the storyteller at work. That is the kind of detail you'll work with as your main character thinks.

Exercises

1. Think of a critically important decision that you or one of your main characters has made or must make. Then write, and use specific details. Be sure that readers can see, smell, and hear, and perhaps taste and touch the place where the decision is contemplated, as well as participate in the thinking process.

2. Study Joyce's story, "Eveline." Then read Tillie Olsen's story, "I Stand Here Ironing," in which a mother irons as she reviews her daughter's problems and what to do about them. Interestingly in "I Stand Here Ironing," the place where the mother irons is not described, very likely because, as we iron, our focus is on the board and the iron, not on our surroundings.

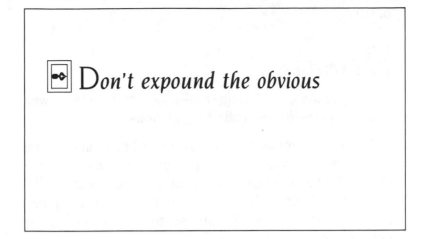

Don't expound the obvious

WE GO TO STORIES TO LEARN SOMETHING NEW. IF YOU FIND yourself writing a wake-up scene in which your character rolls over, reaches for the alarm (which beeps), blinks her eyes against the morning sun filtering through the curtains, yawns, stretches, etc., ask yourself: What's new here? Do I need to write this scene at all? Why am I telling my readers how she wakes up when she wakes up in such an ordinary (and boring) way?

Your readers need to be included in your fictional world, but they don't need to be clobbered with information. They can fill in the blanks themselves. Let them. If you are describing a crowd at a wedding reception, don't describe each person. Neither must you name all the flowers in the arrangement on the food table, or describe all the foods, or give ten examples of how drunken Cousin Booboo is behaving. Instead, focus on the few important details that best reveal the reception and your main character's prejudices and attitudes toward the reception.

Good writers leave a lot out in order to make room for what is new and surprising and interesting in a familiar landscape. In our guide "Reading to Write" we cite bare-bone, taker-outer writers like Carver, Hemingway, and Didion. Learn from them.

Story writing is like sketching. The form is so short that we can include only the most significant, the most revealing details. We sketch the crowd scene, give its bare outlines, highlight a few of the best details, and let the reader fill in the rest.

⊶ Exercises

1. Go through one of your stories looking for places where you've told the reader something obvious. Cut them.

2. Describe a familiar event—waking up, brushing your teeth, fixing lunch, driving a car, shopping for groceries, sitting in church. Leave out most or all of the obvious details; include details that distinguish the character, tell us something about his or her state of mind; surprise the reader with a fresh perspective.

Obvious: The bench was hard, the worn hymnal heavy in her hands. The preacher droned on. Light filtered through the stained-glass window. She looked at the stained-glass shape of Christ on the cross and tried to keep her eyes open.

Not-so-obvious: She sat in the family pew where one Stewart or another had sat every Sunday for the last eighty-five years. She practiced the shoulder squeezes she'd learned in Yoga class: straight back, hands clasped across her stomach, chin up, neck stiff, pressing the shoulder blades together so hard she imagined the bones touching under her sinful flesh.

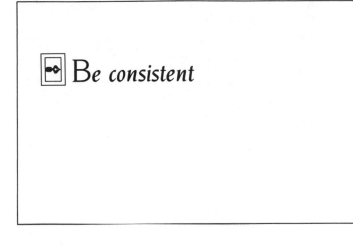

Be consistent

READERS ENTER INTO THE WORLD YOU'VE CREATED ON YOUR pages. They want to believe in the experiences you create for them. Do nothing to interrupt their belief or they'll be jarred out of your story.

Be consistent all through. In your opening paragraph or paragraphs, you lay down ground rules, make a contract with your reader. The rules concern such things as what the story will be about, who the main character is, whether you're using present or past tense, and whether the story will be told in the first or third person.

Readers will believe your ordinary or extraordinary worlds if you develop your story with care and consistency. Be considerate of your reader, who doesn't know your world, who needs a reliable guide. Don't start telling Janine's story and switch without justification on the second-to-last page to Bill's story. Don't start in the past tense and switch to the present without reason. Don't have peony bushes blooming before the snowdrops come out. Create a world readers can believe.

Exercise

Check your stories for inconsistencies. If you have trouble being consistent, read one of your favorite stories and imagine several specific changes that will produce inconsistencies in details or point of view. You'll see how the story loses its power to convince.

STRUCTURE

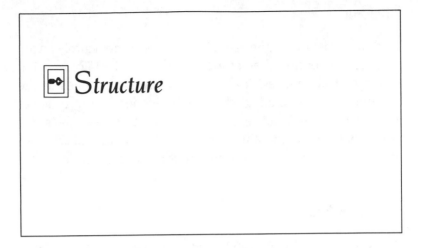

Structure

THE NEXT SEVERAL CHAPTERS CONCERN THE SHAPE, PATTERN, frame, or structure of stories—that is, the way the pieces fit together. This book is structured in a certain way. It's divided into sections, which are divided into chapters, or guides, which are also divided into titles, explanations, and exercises.

In stories, the structure is usually subtle. Sometimes white space indicates a major shift, but in many stories the frame is practically invisible. Readers may be only subliminally aware of structure. After reading the story, if asked how it was set up, many readers might not be able to say exactly. Yet the structure helped them through the story—whether they were conscious of it or not.

After reading Peter Taylor's "The Gift of the Prodigal" for the first time, a reader might not recall that the story is in present tense, that the first couple of pages are a description of Ricky standing in the driveway as he is perceived by his father, that a series of long flashbacks follow, that about four pages from the end the story loops back to the driveway scene with one line, "When Ricky appeared outside my window just now. . . ." The reader might not remember that more flashbacks follow, until finally Ricky comes inside and he and his father talk.

Readers don't have to think a lot about structure; it supports the content of the story without, usually, calling much attention to itself. It's like the studs in the wall—hidden support.

Writers rarely know the structure of their stories before they write. Structure evolves. At some point in the process, though, perhaps most often in revision, writers become acutely aware of structure, of how their stories are designed. Major revision is often structural revision. This may involve changes in the beginning or the ending, changes in scenes or the order of scenes, changes in tense, changes in point of view, decisions about how much time the story will cover and about whether to use flashbacks or to proceed in chronological order.

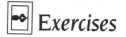 Exercises

1. Read two or three stories, marking scenes, noting where a scene begins and where it ends. Note also how the scenes are connected, what language is used to ease the reader from one scene to another. Does the writer use lots of short scenes, or several short ones followed by a long one? Is the long scene in the beginning balanced by a long scene at the end? Marking scenes is one way to expose a story's structure.

2. Find a story with no flashbacks, that is, no scenes that took place before the main action of the story. Think about why the writer made the choice to begin at point A and move forward chronologically to point B. Find a story with many flashbacks. How does the writer alert the reader that a flashback is occurring? What do the flashbacks add to the story?

3. Analyze a story of your own for structure. Why did you begin and end where you did? Are there other possible beginning and ending points? (If you've written in present tense, try rewriting the first page in past, or vice versa.) What point of view did you choose? What are some other options for point of view? (Try rewriting a section using a different point of view.) Note the sequence of your scenes, the number of scenes, the length of scenes. Consider changes. Do you use flashbacks? If not, would a flashback or two add significantly to the meaning of your story?

When you read like a writer, you become aware of how stories fit together, of the studs beneath the wallboard. Develop the habit of noticing these studs, particularly when you reread. As you learn how good writers design their stories, you will expand your own options.

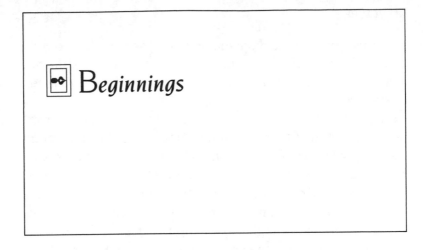

Beginnings

START WITH TENSION OR CONFLICT. READERS ARE BUSY. THEY won't slog through a dull first paragraph. They need a reason to turn the pages—that is, tension and conflict. And you, the writer, need that conflict to hold your interest so you'll keep writing.

Start your story at a place that fascinates you. Start at a crisis point or with a bit of juicy information. If you begin with boring material, by the time you get to the good parts, you'll be exhausted. Your writing will suffer. Remember that after you've begun your story at a strong point, you can always go back and fill in essential background.

Sometimes writers discover their lead after they've worked with the material for a while, after they've explored their characters, their territories.

Read the first paragraphs of ten short stories in an anthology. One right after another. Notice what's accomplished. Notice how many facts and details, how much specific information we are given. Above all, notice how tension or conflict is established.

Writers lay out the ground rules of a story in the lead: Who tells the story? What's the conflict? Readers also get a feeling for the voice of the story, the writer's attitude toward the subject. In a good beginning there is unmistakable authority and we readers feel secure that we're in the hands of a writer who knows the world she's writing about. She won't rely on cheap gimmicks to make us keep reading, such as promising the story will be more dramatic than it is; she won't be coy or withhold essential information. She's a writer who's straightforward, honest. We trust the writer, even if we don't trust her characters.

Write strong leads or your stories will not be read. Editors tell us that if the title and first line grab them, they'll commit to reading the whole first paragraph. If the first paragraph holds them, they will probably read the whole first page. They will put a story down the minute their interest fades or the writer's authority seems questionable. One editor said he reads the title and the first paragraph. If these seem strong, he'll flip to the end. If the ending interests him, he'll read the whole story. All readers make fast decisions about which stories to read and which to skip. You must make those first few lines absolutely fascinating.

Some leads are flamboyant, like the lead to Hilma Wolitzer's "The Sex Maniac": "Everyone said there was a sex maniac loose in the complex and I thought, 'It's about time.'" Alice Walker's very short story "Petunias" begins: "This is what they read on the next to last page of the diary they found after her death in the explosion."

Some leads are subtle but full of tension like this one from "Shiloh" by Bobbie Ann Mason: "Leroy Moffitt's wife, Norma Jean, is working on her pectorals." The sentence raises questions in the reader's mind: Why is she working on her pectorals? What does Leroy think about this activity? Why is this significant—as it must be since it opens the story?

We read leads expecting significance, so writers must take care not to mislead with irrelevancies or false trails. A lead points to the heart of the story.

The Mason paragraph continues with details that draw readers into the scene. Norma Jean starts her workout with three-pound dumbbells and works up to a twenty-pound barbell. Leroy watches her and thinks of Wonder Woman. We see the story is going to be told from Leroy's perspective. We wonder how he feels about Wonder Woman as a wife. There is tension here. It builds and becomes the central conflict.

Toni Cade Bambara starts "The Hammer Man" with this line: "I was glad to hear that Manny had fallen off the roof." She introduces two characters, "I" and "Manny," the title character. The conflict is obvious: Why is the narrator glad Manny fell off the roof? Was he hurt in the fall? Is he dead? What's going on between the two of them?

The second line of Bambara's story gives us dialect and strengthens the voice: "I had put out the tale that I was down with yellow fever, but nobody paid me no mind. . . ." This is a strong voice, magnetic. A personality is emerging fast. By the end of the first paragraph, the narrator's mother has told her that it's bad enough the narrator hangs around with boys, but worse she fights with the "craziest" one of them all. We see a spirited narrator, and also learn something about the mother. This strong tension, this narrator's spirit and voice, draw us into "The Hammer Man."

Usually it's a good idea to pick your readers up by the scruffs of their necks and drop them into the heart of a conflict that has been going on for a long time. But you should also give them the feeling that today—on this special day—something different or more intense is happening to that ongoing conflict. For instance, in "Everything That Rises Must Converge" by Flannery O'Connor, we know that Julian and his mother have been fighting for years. But *on this day* Julian must take his mother to the Y and he does not want to go.

Often your story will start off stronger if you establish a sense of "on this day." Your main character who has been involved in this conflict for some time will now, today, experience an explosion or implosion of some kind. This day is different. Get that sense of a storm about to break going in your story.

Some leads break into the story after the conflict is resolved. The interest shifts from what happened to why and how and what does it mean. For example, a couple dies in a storm at sea. If you start with the bodies being laid out on the dock, the reader's interest shifts from will they survive the storm to who are these people, what happened to them, how did they feel and behave as the storm mounted and they sensed they would die, and what is the significance of their deaths?

Some writers will start a story during the climax scene. Let's use again the example of the couple lost in the storm. A writer could begin his story with the boat tipping over. Then he might go back to when the couple left that morning. The man didn't want to go sailing because of the storm clouds. But the woman had always found her husband stuffy and conservative, and this time decided not to put up with it. We might see how they set off, without life jackets. Soon—or many pages later—the writer could return to the climax, the boat now disabled. After a few pages, or perhaps only a few lines, the characters might die.

Some stories start moments before the climax with the sense of tension about to explode. Still others start where the tension is building but won't erupt for some time.

Some fine stories begin at the start of the action and proceed chronologically.

Some writers are drawn to the straight narrative line. Others like to circle back, creating a loop or many loops.

Where you begin and how you proceed will depend on your temperament and your story. What feels right to you? What will be gained by beginning at the first action or later on? Mull over your options. Or follow your instincts: many writers know very little about their story and characters and can start only with one small piece of information, discovering more as they go along.

Begin at a point that fascinates you. Begin with a character who fascinates you. Begin with a specific conflict, with facts and information. Begin.

⊷ Exercises

1. Read a story you love looking for how it fulfills the promises made in the lead and sticks to the ground rules established there. Think of where else the story might have begun. How would this other beginning change the story?

2. Look at a story of your own. Does it have an effective lead? Is there another paragraph in the story that might work better? Start the story with this new paragraph. What does this lead accomplish? Think about how the rest of the story would change if this were to be your lead.

A good lead is a plunge. Readers are sometimes slightly disoriented by the first couple of paragraphs, but if the paragraphs are clear and make readers want to read on, if the story seems immediately worth telling, the characters worth knowing, readers will be fascinated rather than put off by the momentary shock. The lead must pull readers in by raising questions and offering intriguing details. Avoid deliberately shocking first paragraphs that don't lead to the heart of the story. Readers will stay with a story a good long while if questions are answered, if tension builds, if the promises of the lead are fulfilled.

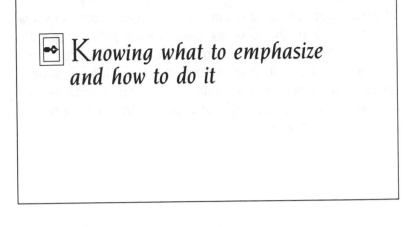

Knowing what to emphasize and how to do it

IN LIFE, THE CLOCK AND OUR SCHEDULES KEEP US MOVING from one appointment to another. Maria is told by her boyfriend in a three-minute phone call that he won't go to her parents' house next week. He's fallen in love with someone else. She's emotionally shaken and needs to talk with him, yet she must rush to school to take her final exam in history, then to the cleaners to pick up her clothes, then downtown to pick up her typed resumés, and on to a friend's house to borrow a briefcase for a job interview.

In a story, we'd want to give the proper emotional weight and space to that telephone call and the few moments following it; we'd play down picking up her clothes and resumés, but would stress how, going out the door of the cleaners, she suddenly begins to cry.

Writers can take control of time and events on their pages as people never can in life. We pace our stories, giving important moments the space they need for full development and impact, skimming or summarizing the rest. We can cover five years in a paragraph—or stretch what happened in one minute over three pages.

The more important the moment, thought, description, or scene, the more space and emphasis writers allot.

Some writers will rush through a first draft knowing they'll come back and write more about this moment, or cut back that one. Other writers may not recognize that something needs to be expanded until a later draft. Perhaps you know what moments you want to emphasize, but you don't yet know how to do it. In the next few guides we'll present specific writing skills to help you control time on your pages. They include writing dramatic scenes (with dialogue, action, thought, description), expanding a critical few moments into a substantial piece of writing, and summarizing a long period of time in a paragraph.

Scenes

A SCENE IS A WONDERFUL WAY TO RENDER A DRAMATIC episode vividly, to give it the emphasis it deserves. A scene allows readers to participate in an experience with all their senses. A scene says to your readers: See here, this is important; pay attention. Scenes slow the pace to allow for in-depth exploration.

We have talked before about how to ground characters when you are exploring their thoughts (as Joyce did in "Eveline"), and how details about characters and their perceptions allow the reader to become involved. Scenes are your opportunity to use these techniques fully.

Some scenes are long descriptions of people and places with almost no dialogue; others rely heavily on dialogue with just a sentence here and there of description. The following advice on writing scenes isn't a recipe. Rather, we present ingredients that are often, but not always, included.

Props and people

When writing scenes, think like an acting director; set up essential props and people. New writers are often told that a director won't cram a stage with furniture and neither should you. But remember that readers will need to see the place in which a dramatic action occurs. Otherwise, as characters talk, their voices will seem to float up from a dark basement. *Ground* your characters. That is, give them ground to stand on, a place to be. Orient your reader with details that help her visualize the scene.

Joy Williams begins her story "Health" by establishing where and when the story takes place. The main character, "Pammy," is riding with her father through the "unpleasant Texas city" where she was born. Williams tells us that Pammy is twelve, that it will soon rain and the rain will "wash the film of ash off the car . . . , volcanic ash that has drifted across the Gulf of Mexico. . . ." She describes the truck on the road ahead, with its "jumble of television sets." She describes one set in particular, "a twenty-four-inch console" with a bullet hole through the screen.

Later in the story, when the father complains that he's tired of driving behind the truck, Pammy thinks "the screen of the injured television looks like dirty water," and the reader is reminded of the opening scene, in all its detail; one quick reference and the reader is re-oriented, is once again in that car with Pammy and her father.

All through your stories, be sure your readers can see.

Often writers will appeal to more than one sense to pull the reader more completely into the moment. Leslie Marmon Silko in "Yellow Woman" embodies a scene by letting the reader look around a cabin at the potbellied stove, the enamel coffee pot, some Navajo blankets. She pulls at other senses with the warmth of the fire, the odor of potatoes frying in the pan, the texture of grease on a character's fingers as he wipes them on his Levis.

Appealing to more than one sense at a time will not only orient your readers but will make scenes more vivid and memorable. After the sense of sight, smell is often the most evocative.

Dialogue

Good dialogue is easy to read. It moves quickly. It does many jobs at once: It brings characters to life, it precipitates action, it reveals background information. Dialogue allows readers to hear what the characters say (engaging the sense of sound as well as our thoughts on what is said); it is often the reader's primary source of information. Good dialogue pushes the story ahead.

Don't use dialogue to spoon feed information but to show how people affect each other's feelings, intellect, guts. Here's an exaggerated example of spoon-fed dialogue: "Look, Carlos, over your head is a spider web which has grown huge because this is an abandoned cellar in which we now stand and I can see clearly that the spider is descending rapidly and may in a moment crawl on your neck."

People don't talk this way. They don't explain where they are to someone who already knows. Just tell readers that Sam and Carlos are in an abandoned cellar with a spider web over Carlos' head. Have Sam point and say "Spider!" or "Look out!"

In life, people often speak in fragments. They repeat words. They start a sentence in a burst of anger and can't finish it. Try to catch these rhythms on the page.

In life, people also spend a lot of time saying things like hi, how are you, I'm fine, how are you. You won't include this small talk in your stories because it doesn't push them forward.

Pay attention to how people talk, but remember that dialogue is not transcription. If you were to record a conversation and include it verbatim in a story, it most likely wouldn't work. It would be too loose, too rambling, too difficult to follow; it would fail to carry its own weight and the reader would quickly become bored. We want to write realistic dialogue, to capture the essence of a conversation, but there is a difference between life and art. When you write dialogue, you're not recording an entire conversation—you're breaking in at critical moments, letting the reader overhear just the good parts. Dialogue has tension. It is dramatic.

Here's an example of dialogue that's filled with tension from Ernest Hemingway's "A Clean, Well-Lighted Place."

"Last week he tried to commit suicide," one waiter said.
"Why?"
"He was in despair."
"What about?"
"Nothing."
"How do you know it was nothing?"
"He has plenty of money."

For many writers, dialogue is easy to draft. One line leads to another. Someone asks a question, the other person answers, and so on. It may help in early drafts to let the dialogue flow, to write pure dialogue without much attribution, without many thoughts or actions between the lines. Then when that's out of your system, boil the dialogue down. In three pages of dialogue you may find just two or three lines that carry their own weight. Keep these. You can add thoughts, actions, commentary, description between these best lines.

Two warnings: Don't let any one character talk too long unless he is terribly worked up. And avoid long dialogues without thoughts, actions, commentary, or description interjected. If your dialogue runs too long, readers will lose their sense of place. They may forget that the scene is set in the kitchen with the peas boiling on the gas stove, in danger of scorching. They may forget the dog whining at the door, or the salesman waiting by the kitchen door.

Without thoughts or actions as guides, readers may miss the significance of the dialogue altogether. Try to balance dialogue with the other elements of scene to keep your reader oriented.

Study the dialogue of Flannery O'Connor and Raymond Carver. In "What We Talk About When We Talk About Love," Carver uses more dialogue than O'Connor and most writers. His dialogue works because it is essential and intense and it moves the story forward: it is the story. Also, the few descriptions he uses are brilliant.

For variety and balance, and to give a sense of a complete conversation without quoting the whole thing, use indirect dialogue: that is, paraphrase what people say without quotation marks. Instead of having Sam say, directly, "That cake looks dumb," paraphrase this way: "Brother Sam had called her mud cake 'dumb' and flattened it with a spatula."

Indirect dialogue can squeeze a lot of information into a short space. Katherine Anne Porter's story "Rope" consists almost entirely of indirect dialogue: "Had he brought the coffee? She had been waiting all day long for coffee." Then, "Gosh, no, he hadn't. Lord, now he'd have to go back. Yes, he would if it killed him." Indirect dialogue can capture the essence of characters' voices without quoting them directly.

In this passage of indirect dialogue from Susan Wheeler's "Hangin' on the Wall," we get the rhythm of Stacey's speech and her tone even though we don't hear her exact words: "Stacey told her husband she'd given the children the spatula as well as a rolling pin and colander and furthermore she would continue to do so. They could have the kitchen sink if they wanted and she wished to God they would take it."

If you do quote directly, rely on *says* or *said* to indicate the speaker, if attribution is needed. Once in a great while you might get away with a *replied* or *shouted* or *asked* or some other short, inconspicuous verb. You want to keep your reader focused on the important quotes rather than on unimportant words that call attention to themselves, such as: responded, retorted, replied, grunted, cajoled, requested, pleaded, cried, begged, exclaimed, exhorted. Readers scarcely notice *says* even when it's used eight or ten times in a row. We're accustomed to it.

Many lines of dialogue stand on their own. Notice that six of the seven lines from "A Clean, Well-Lighted Place" quoted earlier do so. The reader knows who said it and how it was said without explanation from the writer.

Good dialogue doesn't have to be explained. " 'Don't shoot,' he said excitedly." Or " 'Will you go now?' she asked." Obviously he's excited. Obviously she's asking; we can tell from the question mark. Most adverbs that follow a *said* or *says* can be cut. They're either redundant or they're telling what you should be showing. Don't say, " 'I can't go,' she said delightedly." Show her delight. Let us see her expression. And cut the adverb.

Actions and reactions

How people lean forward or draw back from others as they speak, how they stare at their folded hands or glance at their watches or pound the table reveals them and affects other characters.

In "Hangin' on the Wall," Susan Wheeler's main character, Stacey, has lost her temper outside her house, goes inside and her husband, Ned, follows.

> She stood at the picture window in the dining room and stared at the river. Soon Ned was beside her, his face expressionless.
> "Well," he said to the window. "Well, well."
> Stacey glanced at him, his hands in his khaki pockets, his broad shoulders slightly stooped, but no longer the stoop of a person beaten; the stoop of a tall man who doesn't need to swagger. His face was tanned from sailing all summer, his jaw so set and assured that she wanted to slap him. She started for the porch.

Actions and reactions not only help the reader see and understand, but help you—as you write—become immersed in the scene.

Thoughts and feelings

You'll probably want to include some of your main character's thoughts and feelings in important scenes. For example, in Rebecca Rule's story "Lindy Lowe at Bat," Lindy has just stepped up to home plate. Bystanders are shouting for her to whack the ball. The reader knows Lindy's been in a slump and that she's just been fitted with new glasses that may help or hinder her ability to hit the ball. The reader knows her dad is watching. The reader knows her confidence is low. The reader wants to know what Lindy is thinking at this critical moment.

In this case her thoughts may be reported directly: "I'm not afraid of your wicked fast ball, she thought; I am not afraid of you, you big, grinning Belmont pitcher." Or indirectly, and usually this technique creates a more graceful transition from action or dialogue to thought: "Lindy was not afraid of the burly pitcher with the wicked fast ball that, in previous at-bats, blew her away from the plate."

The writer may step in and comment, perhaps saying things about the main character and the situation the character would not say about herself. "Lindy knows what it's like to be hit with a wicked fast ball in the side or the hip or the thigh. The ball-sized black and blue on her rearend is a souvenir of the last game."

These comments fill in background, point up patterns, tell readers how to interpret actions. Mark Helprin and Alice Munro are known for the comments made by their first-person narrators who sometimes comment for paragraphs at a time in stories like "Friend of My Youth" and "Tamar." Remember as you comment in your stories to do it specifically. Don't say: Lindy felt insecure. Or: The pressure was beginning to get to her. Instead, show her adjusting her stance, poking her new glasses into place, remembering or failing to remember the time she hit a triple or the hurtful remark her dad made after the last game.

To get a sense of how different writers set up their scenes, reread some stories you love. Mark each scene—where it begins, where it ends. Look at how individual scenes are constructed, noting descriptions, dialogue, action, reaction, thoughts, and feelings. Look for comments that seem to come from the writer.

It's interesting to note in what proportions different writers use these elements. You'll see that some writers use lots of dialogue with little description. Others rely heavily on description and commentary, with just a touch of direct dialogue here and there. Some writers seem to rely mostly on the surface action and reaction, with almost no mention of the thoughts and feelings of their main characters. Other writers spend most of their time inside their characters' heads, privy to their deepest thoughts and feelings.

Look also at how different writers move from one element to another—from dialogue to description to reaction—and you'll begin to see the ways that scenes fit into a story.

You must decide which events warrant full-blown scenes, which can be summarized, which stretched, and how long each scene should be. These decisions establish the pace of the story and emphasize certain moments over others. They determine not only the shape of your story, but can make the difference between a story that drags and a tense, tight, focused story that keeps readers turning the pages.

▣ Exercises

1. Think of a critically important argument you or one or your main characters has engaged in. Write the argument as a scene, showing the significant characters and the place where the argument occurred. Use dialogue, action, and reaction. Include the thoughts and feelings of the main character. You may also want to comment from time to time on your characters, their actions, their motives. Throughout the scene, be sure your readers can see.

2. Take apart an underdeveloped scene from one of your stories, then put it back together, in an expanded form. Pull out just the lines of dialogue and write them on a clean sheet with lots of space between the lines. Then add action and reaction, then the thoughts and feelings of one of the characters, then props and setting details.

3. Study sections of several stories by different writers. Mark the dialogue, action, reaction, and commentary. How much or how little of each does the writer use? How does the writer shift from action to commentary to dialogue?

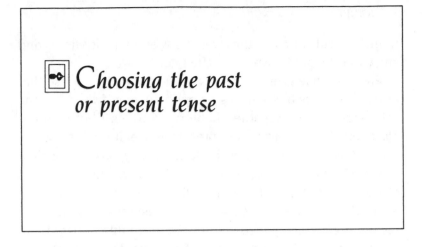

Choosing the past or present tense

YOU MAY SET YOUR STORY IN THE PRESENT AND USE PRESENT tense for the primary action: "I push the mower under the hemlock branches until it just touches the trunk." Or you may set your story in the past and use the past tense for the primary action: "I pushed the mower under the hemlock branches until it just touched the trunk."

When you use present tense for your primary action you may also write of events that occurred earlier by shifting to simple past tense. For example, "I push the mower under the hemlock branches until it just touches the trunk. I mowed behind the garage last week."

When you use past tense for your primary action you may also write of events that happened before the primary action, by shifting into past perfect, using the word "had." "I pushed the mower under the hemlock branches until it just touched the trunk. I had mowed behind the garage last week." "Had" is an alert. It tells readers you are heading back in time.

If the primary action of a story is written in the past tense and if you want to use a long flashback, you can use the word "had" once or twice to establish the time frame, and then use the simple past tense. For example, "I pushed the mower under the hemlock branches until it just touched the trunk. I had mowed behind the garage last week, angry that I had to pick up the branches that had fallen from the hurricane the week before. My brother and sister should have picked up the branches, but they said they were busy studying for finals and knew that I would have to do the work."

Present tense gives your story immediacy and a sense that anything's possible—this is happening now, we're on the roller-coaster ride together, hang on. Carolyn Chute's novel *The Beans of Egypt, Maine* is in present tense. It begins: "We've got a ranch house. Daddy built it. Daddy says it's called 'RANCH' 'cause it's like houses out West in which cowboys sleep in." The strong child's voice lives in the present. Notice, again, the second sentence—a simple past tense statement of something that happened before: "Daddy built it." Then in the third sentence, Chute goes right back into the present with "Daddy says. . . ."

Bobbie Ann Mason writes many stories in the present tense. She's a good writer to study if you want to see how immediate and versatile present tense can be.

Most stories are written in the past tense, that is, they begin and end in the past. The narrator is looking back, telling us what happened (as opposed to what is happening). With past tense, there's a reflectiveness to the writing, a sense of looking back, analyzing, commenting, re-evaluating. There's a sense that something important happened back then, and now, looking back with more detachment, perhaps with wisdom, the story can be told.

⊶ Exercises

1. Choose a story in the past tense and one in the present to read all the way through. Rewrite several paragraphs in each story, switching from past to present or present to past. What difference did the tense choice make in what could be told, and how?

2. Experiment with tense in one of your stories. Rewrite the first two pages of a past tense story to present, or the other way around. As you revise, you'll find that a change in tense means a change in tone, pace, details, and intention.

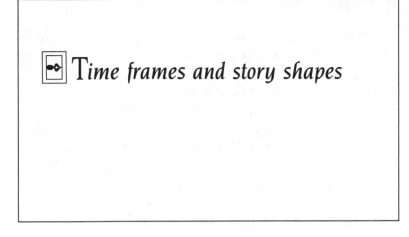

Time frames and story shapes

SOME STORIES TAKE PLACE IN A MINUTE; SOME TAKE years. Ambrose Bierce in "An Occurrence at Owl Creek Bridge" tells the story of a man who is being hanged. The story starts with the noose around his neck. He falls and, while in the air, reviews his life and sees an escape. The story ends with the rope jerking tight and breaking his neck. Although the time of the story is about thirty seconds, the flashback extends over several pages.

Other stories take place over several years, even lifetimes. We pick up a character at this point in time, then the writer skips to an incident several years later, then leaps ahead later still. Alice Munro in "Friend of My Youth" covers many years. It begins with the first-person narrator remembering dreams of her mother long dead, then flashes back to her mother's youth, before the narrator was born, and follows the mother through several years of that youth. By the end of the story, we are back with the narrator in the present.

Faulkner's "Wash" takes place in a day, although years of the main character's life are revealed in the long flashback.

Many writers feel more confident if they know early in the process what the time frame will be—one day, a week, a year. Just as with your choice of where to begin a story, your choice of time frame will be determined, in part, by your sensibilities, your instincts, and your way of seeing the world as well as by the demands of your story. Many of Alice Adams' stories, for example, take place over several years. You may be a person who thinks in years, a person with a long view, sensitive to your characters' histories, interested in cumulative effects, or you may be someone who thinks in flashes, who prefers rendering a short period of time in great detail.

Some people feel more comfortable telling a story that begins at the beginning of a conflict and moves forward one step after another. Writers who think chronologically may prefer to order their stories chronologically. Others would rather start when the conflict erupts in a crisis and use a flashback, returning near the end to that crisis—a loop story. Some begin in the middle of events, flash back, then return to the middle, go forward again, and so forth. Tim O'Brien in the Vietnam War story "The Things They Carried" returns to the death of Ted Lavender again and again in repeating loops. Each time we see the death a little differently and in a little more detail.

One way isn't better than another. Don't use an elaborate structure for the sake of being elaborate. Write as simply and as straightforwardly as you can. Sometimes you'll need to write several drafts before you find the best structure for your story.

⊶ Exercise

Create a time line for a published story you love. Figure out when, chronologically, the story begins. For example, on page five you get a flashback to when the main character is three years old, and on page ten she's getting a divorce at age thirty-seven. The story spans thirty-four years, and the time line begins at "three years old" or "1954" (if you know the year) and ends at "37 years old" or "1988." Number the major scenes of the story (the first scene is "scene 1," the second is "scene 2"), and see where they fall on the chronological time line. (See Figure 1 for this particular example.) This will help you see the shape of the story, the complexities of its structure, and how the writer moves the action forward and backwards in time.

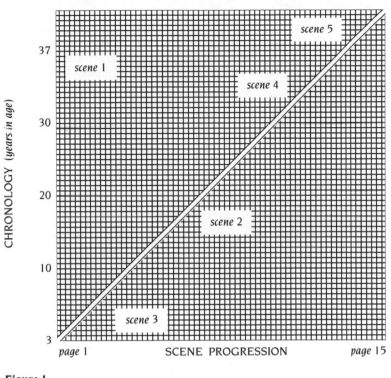

Figure 1

Now try the same analysis on a different story, one that seems much simpler (or much more complex) than the first. You can compare the structures by graphing them.

Now try this analysis on one of your own stories.

Controlling time: Stretches and summaries

Time stretch

A writer may choose to write pages about an important moment of time—one to ten minutes—to give the event its proper emotional emphasis. When you want to stretch a critically important moment or two, think of how television sportscasters replay a high dive in slow motion. That's what you'll do on the page: slow time and examine the moment.

Let's say your main character, Gabor, sees his friend, Pierre, falling through the ice on a lake. It may have taken only a minute or two for Pierre to disappear under the water, but you can write a long paragraph, or even pages about it.

To stretch time, show *the specific sources* of Gabor's fear. This means details. You'll want to rely on the five senses, especially sight. You may also want to comment on what is happening.

Readers will need to know the setting, perhaps a brief description of the lake and who's standing where and doing what. Then you'll show that fall through the ice, very likely through the eyes of the main character.

In life, a number of impressions might reach Gabor at once: the crack of the ice, a cry from Pièrre, knees buckling, a dog barking, hands rising, someone from shore yelling for his dog to come home. Write down one detail after another to create the dominant impression. And always look for distinctive details, not obvious ones.

In her novel *Floating in my Mother's Palm*, Ursula Hegi writes a powerful description of a girl who almost drowns. The story takes place in Germany, and the girl has swum into the middle of the Rhine river and grabbed a steel cable from the stern of a freighter attached to a barge, hoping to be pulled along for the ride. Before she grabs the cable, we see that river—the two barges straining upstream connected by the long cable, puffs of steam blowing from a stack of the first barge. The story is told in the first person, and the narrator tells how she waits for the freighters, treading water, then swims out to find a good spot to grasp the cable. She reaches for it, and then Hegi, stretching time, writes: "The pain was incredible as the skin was torn off my palms. It felt as if the force of the barges straining against the river would tear out my arms. My hands slipped to where the fraying cable disappeared in the current and I was thrust beneath it. I fought to get away, but the cable cut across my stomach and pulled my head underwater." Then the narrator comments: "Somewhere I'd heard your entire life flashes in front of you before you die. Oddly calm, I found myself waiting for that moment, one compact time capsule." The narrator goes on then, to describe her struggle, the cable cutting deeper into her stomach and arms, the "dark pressure" against her ears, the aching in her lungs and eyes, being blinded by yellow dots.

The details bring us into the experience and we understand what happened.

An exceptionally long time stretch occurs in James Agee's novel *A Death in the Family*. Agee writes several pages covering only a few minutes of actual time. The main character, a boy named Rufus, sees his grandmother for the first time. He is told to cross the room, stand close to Grandmother's ear and tell her his name. The woman is ancient, and the experience will affect Rufus for the rest of his life. Agee describes, sensuously, from Rufus' point of view, the woman's wrinkles, her eyes, her ear, even her smell, one impression after another.

Pay attention to how other writers slow time on their pages. Note their most striking details, and how much the writers comment, if at all. In your stories, be alert to moments with potential and do justice to them.

Time summary

You may need to summarize a long period of time in one or more dynamic paragraphs. In a time summary, you'll be exploring important background material that affects your characters. If your story is about a young musician, you might need at some point to summarize his years of practicing. First, think of the major impression you want to convey, such as: Those three years of trumpet lessons were demanding. Then you generate details, facts, examples, anecdotes, and episodes that illustrate the nature of that time period. Choice is important. Of all the details and examples you can think of, which are best? (Look at our guide, "Use Distinctive Details.")

Many writers like to write a summary quickly, then revise, substituting stronger details and examples as they think of them. Here is an excerpt from a time summary from Susan Wheeler's story "Hangin' on the Wall." It covers three years and seven months when a man's job was threatened and finally lost. It is from his wife's perspective.

> During the three years his job had dribbled away, and even during the seven months he was out of work, he had slept like an innocent, while she, night after white night, stared at the ceiling, listened to his breathing: maddening, oblivious. At 11:30 or midnight she would go to the livingroom, turn on the lights, prop herself against pillows on the low yellow couch. She could not bear music. Not even Bach. The New York Times, the Maine Times, E.B. White, Legends of the Maine Coast—they did not work. Nor did vodka and beefamato juice. In May she had begun rolling the TV into the livingroom.

In this piece a few carefully chosen details allow the reader to generalize, to gain an impression of what was going on with this character over a long, painful period, to feel the impact of that experience.

Some writers begin their stories with a time summary or overview of a situation or character. Then they zoom in on one particular time in the character's life. D.H. Lawrence's "The Rocking-Horse Winner" begins with a time summary: "There was a woman who was beautiful, who started with all the advantages, yet she had no luck." We learn that she married for love, which had "turned to dust," that she had children, but couldn't love them. We learn where the family lived and the style in which they lived. We learn that the family had long been plagued by a shortage of money. Then a page and a half into the story, the main action begins with a scene between mother and son in which they discuss the connection between money and luck.

Other stories that open with time summaries include Ursula Hegi's "Saving a Life," Saul Bellow's "Leaving the Yellow House," and Anne Whitney Pierce's "Sans Homme."

Time summaries allow you to concentrate on the most important material of your story without slogging through pages of history that could be condensed.

⊶ Exercises

1. To practice stretching time, think of a one-to-ten-minute experience that's etched in your memory or in the memory of one of your main characters. For example, waiting for the curtain to rise on a play in which your character has a main part, seeing a man you love with another woman, watching a respected colleague or a parent, drunk, make a fool of himself or herself. Then think of the dominant impression you want to create. Write the details that produced the dominant impression. Render the experience in a sensuous way. Rely on the five senses, especially sight.

2. To practice summarizing time, think of a long period—a month to several years—that you or a character feel strongly about: for example, five years of brutal football practices, your first marriage, years of family gatherings at Thanksgiving. Think of the dominant attitude your character has toward this period. Then write details to illustrate the nature of that time.

You may want to comment as well, but be sure you create a sensuous experience to support the comments.

You must decide which events warrant stretching on your pages and which need to be summarized. These decisions will be based on what you are trying to say, that is, theme and meaning, which we cover in the guide "Finding Meaning."

⊡ Moving characters from one time and place to another

BE CLEAR ABOUT WHERE YOUR CHARACTERS ARE IN TIME AND place. Don't wait five lines into a paragraph to establish this. Be clear at once. When you're fuzzy, readers, instead of concentrating on your character and what is happening, will be trying to figure out whether your characters are in an apartment or an elevator and whether this conversation took place weeks or days after the last scene.

When you move your characters, move them fast. Novelist Mark Smith tells students there is nothing wrong with saying, "Four years later, in Montreal. . . ."

Years ago writers took more time getting people from room to room, from one place in time to another. Now, partly because of television, we're used to abrupt scene and time shifts. When your scene has accomplished what it needs to, stop. Start a new paragraph with your character in a new room. You don't need to write that transition paragraph in which your character stands, puts on her coat, buttons it, opens the door, goes out, and closes the door, unless these actions have direct bearing on the heart of the story.

If you're leaping ahead two years and going from Mexico City to Duluth, consider a space break. Space breaks alert your readers to a significant shift. A phrase or two may be all you need to alert the reader to the new setting. For instance, Jeff, a beginning teacher, discovers that his favorite student, Max, has cheated on an exam. He worries over what to do. He tries to talk with Max about it, but the conversation goes badly.

You can write that awkward scene between Jeff and Max. Then you can say, "Later that day, as Jeff sat alone in his small study, he thought about. . . ."

As we discussed in "Time Frames and Story Shapes," you may want to follow a character's growing awareness of conflict over a long period. You can show what he thinks at one point in time, show that thought changing weeks or years later in another place, and show it change again still later. For instance: Later that day, as he sat alone in his small study, he thought_____. The next day, it seemed to him that_____was true. But it wasn't until two years later, at graduation, as he watched Max march in with the others to receive their diplomas that he realized_____.

Yuko Tsushima in "The Silent Traders" makes dazzling time and place shifts. Several connected scenes involve the Rikugien wood, a walled landscape garden in the city. The story begins as a mother and her children discover wild kittens in the Rikugien. Then Tsushima flashes back twenty-five years to the mother's childhood experiences with the Rikugien: a visit with classmates to bury a time capsule; then, in high school, the death of her pet dog, its replacement with a puppy, and the subsequent abandonment of the troublesome puppy over the wall of Rikugien. Tsushima moves the story through time with simple, clear phrases: "It is exactly twenty-five years since . . . ," "I visited Rikugien with several classmates when we were about to leave elementary school . . . ," "While I was in high school. . . ."

You can start your story, as Tsushima does, in the middle of a sequence of events, then go backward and forward. The only rule is: Be clear.

◄► Exercises

1. Check the stories you've written recently to be sure readers know at once where your characters are.

2. Read John Cheever's story "Torch Song" which is in his collection of short stories. This traces the relationship of a

man and woman over a fairly long period of time. Notice how in each time shift, Cheever lets readers know exactly where the characters are in time and place.

3. Study Toni Morrison's *Song of Solomon* for time shifts. Mark the phrases she uses to alert the reader that a shift in scene is about to occur, or already has. Or choose any story you like with a complex time frame and mark the time-shift phrases to see how the writer helps the reader stay on track.

Flashbacks

FLASHBACKS ARE WONDERFULLY USEFUL. YOU CAN BEGIN your story at a dramatic moment, rather than plodding through dull background material. When readers are thoroughly engaged, then you can go back in time and deliver essential information that they should know.

As you write a story, you may feel the need at some point to explore something in a character's past. For example you may want to develop specific facts about a character's first job or a weight problem he struggled with in his teens. Through this exploration, you may discover how your character sees his world, how he makes sense of it, or fails to. You may learn the specific workings of a character's mind, observe his mental wheels turning on a problem he once faced.

Other times you will already know the specific facts and decide to dramatize them in a flashback or you may decide to tell them in a factual, straightforward way.

Flashbacks help you and the reader to understand things in context. If you're writing about a relationship between two people, you probably don't want to start with their amicable meeting at a dance. Very likely you'll begin at a point of conflict when, for example, they're having a fight. Later you and your reader may need to know how long they've known each other and you can use a flashback. After all, if two people have only just met, a fight won't have the same meaning as it would if they've been lovers for eight years.

In Ethan Canin's "Emperor of the Air," a long flashback to the main character's childhood begins several pages into the story: "When I was a boy in this town. . . ." Canin flashes back over fifty years to a terrible fire, a fire that almost took the main character's home, a fire that taught him something about his family and himself and permanence. He had watched the fire for a while from the branches of an ancient elm tree in his yard. The main action of the story concerns that same elm tree, now diseased, and the main character's fight to save it from a neighbor who wants it cut down. Through the flashback we learn a lot about why that tree is so important to the main character.

A good flashback delivers only essential information that informs the present action of the story, that pushes the story ahead, and that adds to the main character's burden. In early drafts especially, go back in time to find out for yourself about your characters. Allow yourself to delve in deeply. Even if you decide to throw out some or all of what you learn, the information will help. It will give you authority and confidence.

Be sure when you head into and emerge from a flashback that readers know where you are in time and place. Some writers use space breaks when they go into a fairly long flashback. At the end of the flashback, they'll break again. Richard Selzer in "The Masked Marvel's Last Toehold" indicates a shift in time three ways before a long flashback. He writes "and I remember . . ." to show reflection; he uses a space break, and then he opens the flashback with "It is almost forty years ago," so the reader knows precisely when the events are taking place.

Many writers use the word "had" to indicate they're heading back in time. They may use a change in tense (from simple past to past perfect) in addition to space breaks, or they may use a change in tense and omit space breaks. "Had" is an alert. It tugs at the reader's sleeve and says, I'm going back in time. For long flashbacks, some writers will use the word "had" two or three times right away to establish the flashback, then continue in the simple past.

If you're writing in the present tense, you don't need "had" to indicate a flashback; the simple past tense will do; for example, from Rebecca Rule's story "Wood Heat, No Backup": "Tom complains that some of the wood I brought in to fill the stove is too long, doesn't fit. *We started* the winter with three cord of dry wood and a cord or so of semi-dry. The first snow came before Thanksgiving, before the roof struts over the addition were even in place." Because the primary action is in present tense, the slip into past tense (*we started*) indicates a flashback.

Before you go back in time, leave readers with memorable, essential details at a memorable, essential place in the story— one they'll recognize when you return to it. For example, if a character has insulted someone at a party and recognizes she's been cruel and stupid, and if she rushes to the bathroom, ashamed, you might want to have her reflect on other times she's lost control. You could have her stare in the mirror. Then have her reflect on her past temper outbursts, perhaps trying to understand her behavior. At the end of this flashback sequence, you return to the mirror maybe showing her eyes which she sees are full of fear.

Flashbacks can be as short as a sentence or they can be the longest part of your story. They can include dramatic scenes with dialogue, time stretches, or summaries. They can include commentary on characters and events, or offer a straight-forward account of what happened.

A warning: New writers sometimes start a story and fail to ground readers in the present action before flashing back to the past. They may write just one or two lines before heading into background material. Let's say a story begins this way: "He stood on the dock and watched the boat that was about to capsize." Then comes a long flashback into what happened before—who the passengers are, how they came to be in this predicament on the boat, what their relationships are. This transition into a flashback without first establishing a memo-rable scene will confuse readers. Lacking strong details to make the danger stick in their minds, readers won't care as much as they should about the capsizing boat, will wonder why they are given so much background information, and, after they've read the flashback, may even forget that the boat had capsized.

Let your readers know what's what and who's who in an opening scene. Hook them thoroughly; then, when they know what's at stake, are involved, and have a reason for reading on, you can go back in time.

When introducing a flashback, it is usually unnecessary to say, "She remembered back to a time when. . . ." Often a character does not remember back to that specific time; rather, it's the writer filling in information. So don't be dishonest and claim a memory your character's not experiencing or readers will smell rats and mistrust you. Instead, start a new paragraph and say something like, "Bill had stood on this same rock last fall and. . . ."

Here are a few phrases writers use to move into flashbacks. There are hundreds of ways to make transitions; you'll find your own in each story.

- Often she had thought that . . .
- She hadn't realized that . . .
- Earlier, she had believed . . .
- In Kansas last summer he had . . .
- It sometimes seemed to him . . .
- He used to . . .
- Whenever he thought about Sam . . .
- For three years she had . . .
- Lately she had . . .
- When she had been in high school . . .
- In those days he had . . .

Exercises

1. Write from the point of view of someone you've had a fight with about something important to both of you. Start with one or two vivid paragraphs when the crisis erupts. Then leave a space break and go back to find out how the other person thought about and made sense of the issue leading up to the fight. What were the character's reasons for acting as he or she did?

2. Think of a time in your life when you were duped. Almost all of us have had that experience. First, write a few paragraphs about the time you became convinced you had been duped. Then go back in time and show the history of the ways your perceptions developed. Use the third person. Be specific. You may want to use some short scenes, or dwell for a long paragraph or two on one critical moment, combining these with summaries. You may want to step in and comment—say something that you, earlier, might not have been able to say or see about yourself. Whatever means you use, render this background information vividly, specifically.

3. Write about a critical event, set in the past, from the point of view of someone you know (or a character based on someone you know) who has a strange way of seeing something: for instance, someone who's very superstitious and takes everything as an omen, or someone who is so insecure he feels everyone is out to get him, or someone who's very gloomy or aggressive or passive. Start with a specific conflict that has been precipitated by his strange views. Then try to discover, in a flashback, how that person's mind clicks along and comes to conclusions. Render this in a detailed, dramatic way.

4. Take a character you've written about and show how she has viewed another person, herself, a situation, or a conflict over a long time period. Go as deeply as you can into the character's mind. Show its workings; show the machinery ticking as she tries to make sense of things. Does this addition enrich your story? If so, keep it. If not, throw it out.

How to reveal important information

HANDY AS IT WOULD BE, YOU CAN'T USE A KNOWLEDGE NEEDLE to inject your reader all at once with everything she needs to know about your characters, their situations, their backgrounds. The world of the story grows in increments, detail by detail. Many beginning writers make the mistake of lumping background information somewhere in the story, often in the lead. Instead of leading with background information, much of it unnecessary, and most of it lacking tension, begin with a scene or with one fascinating fact. You'll find you won't include nearly as much irrelevant information this way.

Showing is more dramatic than telling. But telling is more efficient than showing. Good stories show *and* tell. The trick is knowing when to do which.

Important background information should be delivered smoothly; often it can be evenly distributed throughout the story, leaving no lumps. Here is an example of a lumpy lead that includes too much irrelevant background information:

> Shirley and Carol had known each other for seven years, ever since Shirley had moved to town with her husband, Jeff, and their three children. Lori, blond and fat, was six at the time. Jeff Junior was four and full of terrible energy. And P.J. was a baby. They moved into a fifteen-room Victorian across the street from the eighteenth-century cape where Carol had grown up.

Some of this information may become important later in the story. At that point when the reader wants and needs to know these facts, they can be reported directly—one fact after another, no apologies, no fluttering about. Your readers will be grateful. But here, lumped in the beginning before the reader cares about the characters, before the story has even begun, the information is boring.

Sometimes, however, when you need to inform your reader of critical background material, rather than tucking it in here and there, it's better to deliver it in a few information-packed sentences. Bobbie Ann Mason in the sixth paragraph of "Shiloh" does this. In that paragraph we learn that Leroy is a truck driver and that he injured his leg four months ago. Now he lifts weights for physical therapy. He's collecting disability. We are told he's frightened about going back to work. To keep himself busy he's made things from craft kits. Mason could have slipped this information in over the course of the whole story, but we need to know these facts right away, so she delivers them fast.

Never withhold essential information to be clever or to lure the reader on. Readers want to be lured by their interest in characters and the characters' complexities, not by superficial curiosities.

As the story develops, you'll want to add essential background as it is needed. This means information that gives us insight, adds to or reveals the burden of your main character, and increases the tension, the forward motion, and the meaning of your story.

How do you know what's essential? Often in first drafts you don't. Many writers will write what they need to know, what feels relevant at the time, later deciding what to keep. Ask yourself: how does this information contribute to the forward motion of the story, to my main character's burden, to the theme? What would be lost if I were to leave it out?

In Grace Paley's story "The Pale Pink Roast," a divorced husband and wife are reunited for an afternoon at her new apartment. They talk, and then later, they have sex; the story explores hope and love. Not until the end of the story do the husband and, at the same time, the reader discover that the wife has remarried. This information could have been revealed at any point in the story, but Paley revealed it when it needed to be revealed. The wife deliberately withholds information from the husband, allowing him to make love to her in the apartment where she'll live with another man, her new husband. The revelation of her remarriage brings the story to a dramatic conclusion.

In Rebecca Rule's "Heritage" two lovers walk through the woods. Gradually readers learn that the lovers are walking near the woman's family homestead, that the homestead burned years ago, that only the cellar hole remains. They come upon the two granite "steps to nowhere" that once led to the front door. Readers learn that the woman's grandfather had been born in this place, that her great-grandmother had died young, and that her portrait was one of the treasures rescued from the fire.

The woman's deep connections with this place gradually become clear as does her affection for her lover and her uncertainty about their future. The story ends with an "if-then" proposition in the mind of the woman "I," and one final revelation as they lie together in the moss: "If my lover is gentle and considerate, if he acknowledges—with a breath, a touch, a respectful word—the sanctity of this place, I will show him her grave in the hollow beyond the birches. The stone that bears my name."

The gravestone with her name on it could have been described in the first paragraph, or any other, as background information. To save it for the end is to give the stone special significance and to allow it to pull the emotional threads of the story together.

◄► Exercise

Read a story aloud in sections, a paragraph at a time or a page at a time depending on length. (Mary Robison's story "Yours" and Charles Baxter's "The Cliff" work particularly well for this exercise, but any strong story under five or six pages will do.) After each section consider what of significance has been revealed about the characters and their situations. Speculate about what will happen next in the story. Then read on to see how your expectations are met or altered by new information.

Pay attention to how information is revealed: through dialogue, through description, through thoughts or actions, or through narrator commentary.

What does the writer tell us directly? What does the writer show us?

Play around with the order in which you reveal information. This is not a matter of withholding information in order to spring it on readers: that's contrived and manipulative. This is simply deciding what order makes sense if your story is to hold its tension and fulfill its dramatic potential. Decide what to reveal, when to reveal it, and how.

Sudden fiction and short-entry stories

WRITERS SPEND A LOT OF TIME DEVELOPING CHARACTERS, building scenes, filling them in, choosing the most revealing details. Through detail and commentary writers probe the lives of their characters. This is a tradition of the short story.

On the other hand, some wonderful stories break with tradition. They have bare-bones scenes or non-scenes that dazzle the reader by coming on strong and fast. Many of these stories, some very short, have been collected by Robert Shepard and James Thomas in their *Sudden Fiction* anthologies. In some of these stories characters are underdeveloped but striking. Some of the stories are mostly characterization with just a hint of plot. Some are descriptions with slight, subtle movement toward crises. They have one thing in common though: something happens. There is a change, however slight, in a character's situation or perception.

Maybe you know the stories we mean. They break somebody's rules of what a short story is supposed to be, but adhere fast to their own; they hit you hard.

Stories like "Girl" by Jamaica Kincaid—one long sentence broken only by semicolons, moving from command ("Wash the white clothes on Monday . . .") to statement ("this is how to sew on a button") to question ("you mean to say that after all you are really going to be the kind of woman who the baker won't let near the bread?").

Stories like "Lust" by Susan Minot—a series of quick commentaries on the relationships of the main character. She writes, in brief, about Leo, Roger, Bruce, Tim, Willie, Phillip, and Eben: "Tim's line: 'I'd like to see you in a bathing suit.' I knew it was his line when he said the exact same thing to Annie Hines." And through this series of short entries, the reader comes to understand the narrator and her feelings about sex and herself.

Stories like "Roselily" by Alice Walker, each short section introduced by a phrase from the wedding vow: "Dearly Beloved," the story begins, "If there's anybody here that knows a reason why," introduces section five.

In many of these stories, the structure dominates, that is, structure is what readers notice first and last; it's the most obvious element; it seems to define the story. As a writer, once you have such a structure in mind, you can run with it and see what happens.

These stories are interesting to write.

They are fun to read.

Try one.

▣ Exercises

1. Sit down at your desk to write a complete story in one sitting. Time yourself. Allow yourself no more than, say, three hours to create as finished a story as you can. Try to keep the story under five pages.

2. Imitate a very short story. Write a story like Jamaica Kincaid's that is one long sentence, mostly commands and directions, connected by semicolons. Or a story like Susan Minot's that uses a series of short specific examples to illustrate a concept. Or a story like Alice Walker's that incorporates familiar language (like the wedding vow or the Pledge of Allegiance or the Mr. Ed theme song) with new language.

Every story has ground rules. These rules are established by the middle of page one: rules about point of view, pace, tone, territory, character, structure. In some stories—especially sudden fiction—the rules may be particularly obvious. Writing very short stories is an efficient way to experiment with different rules and form; it is a way to develop flexibility.

As for imitating stories, in a sense all writing is imitative. Writers learn about choices from the stories they read. If you call on your own experience and attitudes in your imitation, no one will care where you got the idea for structure. Or if they do recognize the source, they'll probably be amazed by their own insight and impressed by your knowledge of literature.

Endings

AN ENDING WILL OFTEN REVEAL ITSELF TO YOU. THIS MAY take several drafts, but if you've written one clear, honest sentence after another, and paid attention to each word and to its meaning, you will most likely come upon an insight, a revelation, or an action that will end your story. It's a good idea not to worry about the ending too much until you've written several drafts.

A good ending is the culmination of everything that comes before. It emerges from the heart of the story and adds something new. It isn't a summary of what's happened nor is it a moral lesson. A good ending should not snap shut like a pocketbook, allowing the reader to go off and think about something else. Ideally an ending makes the reader want to weave his way back through the story, reflecting on it.

Often the ending is an illumination, an insight, or a piece of wisdom that strikes the writer and reader—something earned but also something of a gift. And yet the groundwork for your gift has been your own careful writing.

An ending often seems to rise above the story.

The last line of James Joyce's "The Dead," for example, rises above the concerns of the particular characters, whose relationships have been so carefully developed. The main character, Gabriel, looks out his window on the falling snow and reflects on his relationship with his wife, sleeping nearby, and on her tragedy: the death of her young lover years before. In the final sentence, Joyce moves dramatically and poetically—

through repetition, generalization, and simple, beautiful language—from the particular, to the universal: "His soul swooned slowly as he heard the snow falling faintly through the universe and faintly falling, like the descent of their last end, upon all the living and the dead."

Endings resolve what's gone on before. Sometimes the resolution is embodied in an action. Sometimes it is represented by an image. Sometimes the character or the writer comes to an insight. Sometimes an ending doesn't seem much like an ending until you think about it. Sometimes the resolution is that there will be no resolution, just a slightly enhanced understanding of the characters and their world.

Some endings may be essay-like commentaries, new awarenesses, insights that grew from the careful detail of the story.

Some endings continue the action of the story and give us new information and details right up to the last line. In Richard Selzer's "The Masked Marvel's Last Toehold," even the last line is a physical action and the story ends in the middle of surgery. This is a story in three sections. Section one: an encounter between the main character, a surgeon, and the wrestler after the wrestler's left leg has been amputated. The surgeon recognizes Elihu Koontz as The Masked Marvel. Section two: a long flashback to one of The Masked Marvel's wrestling matches that made a big impression on the surgeon when he was a boy. Section three: the amputation of the wrestler's right leg.

When Elihu Koontz wrestled, he wore a mask. Now the surgeon wears the mask. Now he wears his gown and gloves. Now fluid drips and needles pierce the Masked Marvel's skin. The orderly holds up the leg that is to be removed and the intern paints it. The surgeon remembers the wrestling match he'd watched years before and his Uncle Max yelling: "Tear off a leg. Throw it up here." We are deep in the surgeon's mind. Selzer writes: "And I think that forty years later I am making the catch."

" 'It's not fair,' I say aloud. But no one hears me. I step forward to break the Masked Marvel's last toehold."

Insight, in this case, is followed by action and the story is over.

Beware the boomerang ending that flies at you from an unexpected direction and takes unpredictable, unjustified twists and turns. Don't introduce a whole new element at the last minute. For instance, a writer tells of a teenager who steals wallets at school. The conflict mounts and is resolved by the last-page introduction of a rich uncle who takes the boy to a farm in Kansas and provides meaning and stability in his life. The classic boomerang ending to many young children's stories is: "and then the house burned down and they died."

As we mentioned, before, you needn't know—and perhaps it's better not to know—the ending before you start your story or even know it for sure after a rough draft or two. It's fine if you think you know how things *may* turn out, it's comforting to be writing in the direction of an image or event, but don't force characters into ways of thinking and acting to accommodate that ending. This will make them stiff and produce a shallow story. Instead, hold that ending in an open palm; let go of it the minute you feel yourself pushing your characters about.

If you're having trouble with an ending, most often the trouble is not with the ending but with the rest of the story. Check yourself: Have you written one clear, honest sentence after another? Is the story focused? Are your characters fully developed? Are the details adding up to something significant? Are there moments of insight in the story that can lead you to a final revelation or conclusion?

Often writers find they can cut the last paragraph or two or three from their stories. They find they have overshot their endings. Ask this of your final paragraphs: Is each one advancing my story? Is there new action or insight? Beware stating what readers already know.

Endings are apt to sneak up on writers. Writers will be writing along when, wonderfully, out will come a paragraph that sounds like an ending and it is.

◄► Exercises

1. Read the last few paragraphs of your three favorite stories. See what each accomplishes and how. Pay attention to how the ending grows out of everything that came before. Pay attention to the careful language and think about why the writer chose these words, particularly for the last sentence.

2. Go back to one of your stories in which the ending doesn't work. Read the story all the way through. Edit or revise each section, line by line, word by word (that is, immerse yourself in the story), and see if a new ending—or an inkling of a new ending—doesn't present itself to you.

Boomerang endings try to solve all the problems at once, to tie up all the loose ends; they try to do too much and so are unearned and unbelievable.

Resist, too, the temptation of an easy resolution that doesn't fit your story. One of our students wrote about two roommates in love with the same man. She wrote wonderfully detailed, realistic scenes showing the roommates' conflict. The point of view character agonized about destroying a friendship over what might turn out to be a crush. Did she really love the man? Did he have any interest at all in her? Could she compete with her beautiful roommate? Was a relationship with him worth losing her best friend?

She didn't know what to do. The writer was stumped, too. So she invented a fairy godmother who appeared in the kitchen on the last page and granted the woman's wish for the man to love her instead of her roommate.

In subsequent drafts, the writer canned the fairy godmother and worked instead on figuring out what the character really would do, how she really would feel and her character faced reality.

How much more interesting it is to have a character cope with problems, successfully or unsuccessfully, than to summon a fairy godmother. (Unless your story is a fairy tale or fantasy from the first—unless fairy godmothers are part of the reality you've created.)

Point of View

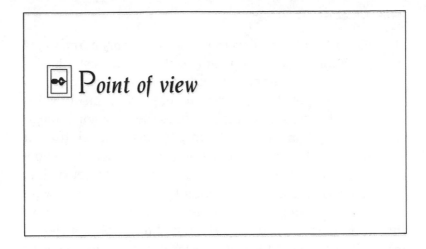

Point of view

WHOSE STORY DO YOU WANT TO TELL? DO YOU WANT TO TELL the story of your main character and say "he" or "she" did this and thought that? Or do you want to use the first person and write "I" did and thought this and that? Do you want to get inside the head of your main character and stay there, showing only what he sees, hears, touches, thinks, and feels, or do you want to distance yourself sometimes and record how he looks as he walks down a street? Or do you want to get into the minds of several characters? These are a few of your point-of-view options.

First, we'll describe a situation to show what storytellers mean by point of view. Let's pretend the following event happened to you when you were fourteen years old, and you want to write about it, changing it so that it takes on a life of its own. Your mother, father, and brother went to a small cabin on Moosehead Lake for a weekend of ice fishing. Your mother believed the ice was not frozen enough to walk on. Your father insisted it was safe, but he warned all of you to stay a good twenty-five feet behind him as he set out, "just in case." He was close to a small island near the middle of the lake when the ice gave, and he went under and drowned.

Whose story will you tell? Your father's? Your own? Your mother's or brother's? Each character's point of view is worth telling. You could even tell the story from everyone's point of view, describing what the mother saw and felt as the father walked onto the ice, what the girl was thinking and saying as she followed her father, how the father was angry at the warnings of his wife, how the son felt about his older sister insisting that she walk in front of him and their mother.

To decide what point of view to use, ask yourself which character interests you the most, causes the most adrenalin to run in your system, and which story is close enough to your experience so that you can draw on the details, information, and relationships you need in order to write with conviction. Since we'll say you are the daughter here, and you know what it is like to be a daughter, and a sister, and presuming you know this world of ice fishing, then the daughter's point of view is most likely the best for you to use, especially in your first stories. Let's say that you choose the daughter's point of view—and notice we're already urging you to get distance on this by calling you "the daughter." Do you want to become that girl and write from the first-person point of view, using the word "I"? In this case you might write, "I watched, stunned, as my father fell. . . ." Or will you use third-person point of view and say, "She watched, stunned, as her father fell. . . ." You may, like many writers, decide that you can get more objectivity on a character based on yourself when you use the third person.

Always, as you make point-of-view choices, think of yourself. You are the writer. Your temperament and character and needs are critical to your choice. You must have conviction and enthusiasm for the point of view you choose. Think also of your main character, of her conflict, of what you sense to be the movement of your story. Because you need to write using believable facts and details, pick a character and situation you can write about with authority. Then, knowing the point-of-view options and some of the demands of your story, pick the viewpoint that feels right for your story and right for *you*.

Immediately, we think of exceptions. We know several writers who have published stories in which they didn't consider what point of view to use. The choice seemed made for them. They started writing and found themselves saying "I" or "he." However, these writers knew a lot about point of view. In most of their stories they had thought about which was the best to use.

Another consideration for writers when they think about point of view is distance: where they stand in relation to their characters. We encourage you to think of yourself as holding a camera and recording what your characters do and say. You can stand far away from your characters and take long shots, or stand close to them. This is a magic camera. You'll be able to select details carefully since you would never want to record every detail. The camera is magical in another way: it can enter people's minds and reveal their thoughts and feelings. And the camera can even get right behind your main character's eyeballs and see exactly what your character sees.

For instance, in the story "Everything That Rises Must Converge," which we have referred to before, Flannery O'Connor has chosen to tell the story from Julian's point of view, with the third person, "he." This is Julian's story. He's finished college and still lives at home. The story opens with his having to take his mother to the Y for reducing class and he doesn't want to go. Let's say that O'Connor the writer is holding her camera recording what happens. First, O'Connor holds it a little to one side of her two characters so we see Julian and his mother in the front hall, see Julian watching his fat mother put on a hat. We see that hat too: it is ridiculous. Then O'Connor turns the camera full on Julian and we see how he responds to the hat: he puts his hands behind his back " . . . like Saint Sebastian about to receive the arrows," and, martyr-like, rolls his eyes to the ceiling.

O'Connor is flexible in the way she uses her camera. Sometimes she'll pull way back, as when she describes during their walk to the bus stop, the street Julian and his mother live on. We see that shabby street vividly with its dirty brownstones. Then the camera moves right into Julian's mind and we see how he regards the neighborhood, what it means to him. After this, O'Connor pulls the camera out of his head and holds it near the mother and Julian, recording their argument. At one point the mother talks about her once rich relatives and the family mansion, now dilapidated. We see and hear the mother talking about this, and then the camera moves into Julian's head again and we learn how he yearns in his fantasies and dreams for those days when the family had money and how he loves the "threadbare elegance" of the house more than anything he can name. Because of the mansion, every place he and his mother have since lived in has been a "torment to him." Right after this insight O'Connor pulls the camera from inside Julian's head, steps back a few paces, and lets us see both characters, walking along, arguing. Later in the bus Julian sits across from his mother and O'Connor gets her camera right behind his eyeballs so we see exactly what he sees as he stares at his mother, noting specific things about her that disgust him.

As we discuss point of view in O'Connor's story, we're considering two things: (1) Whose story this is. (It's Julian's. The writer stays with Julian's story, and we readers see what Julian sees, know what he knows, and thinks and feels.) And: (2) Where O'Connor stands with her camera in relation to her main character. (She's all over the place.)

It's fascinating to read that story and pay attention to her camera placement at each moment, watch her extraordinary agility. Throughout the story she lets us see outstanding details that her main character notices and that she wants us to see, and she keeps going back into Julian's head, sometimes for just a phrase or sentence, sometimes for a paragraph, so we know how he regards what is happening. That camera reveals people and place, and records conversation brilliantly. O'Connor also pulls the camera way back and says things about Julian he could never say about himself.

You can do this too. Think in terms of camera lenses: panoramic, zoom, and in-between, as well as the magic part where your camera can enter a character's mind, explore what he's thinking, and get right behind his eyeballs, see precisely what he sees. You can go into a person's head for pages, not at all, or now and again. You can pull back the camera and comment on the character, giving the reader insights the character could never have about himself.

As you read stories, pay attention to different points of view and to what each can and cannot accomplish.

Here is a brief discussion of some of your point-of-view options.

Omniscient: Unlimited

You are God. You can even choose what kind of god you want to be. For instance, you can go into every character's head and you can know things and can tell the reader things that no one knows or only some people in the story know. You can comment in a phrase, a sentence, or at length on your characters' behavior or their ways of thinking.

Or you can decide to limit yourself somewhat, and you can reveal the events of the story as though you were a movie camera taking panoramic shots along with some close-ups, but never go into anyone's mind. You can limit yourself in other ways. You can decide that you want to follow only two characters and to go into their minds, but not into the minds of minor characters. You might decide to tell the readers things that neither of your two characters know; then again, you might limit yourself to revealing only what these two characters know. Or three characters. Or all of your characters.

You can be a flexible god. At the beginning of the story, you might choose to be a very distanced god, telling how this group of people did this and how that individual did or said that, and then, if it suits the demands of your story and your instinct about what's right, you can zoom in to a close up and follow one character for a while, even getting into her deepest thoughts, yearnings, and secrets, and then pull back again to show an overview that may include events and ideas of which your character is unaware.

By going into more than one character's perspective in a story, you risk confusing the reader, so you have to be clear and smooth about this. More seriously, you risk being superficial. Stories are short. If you go into the heads of two or more characters you can't go in very deeply because you haven't much space, whereas in a novel you would have hundreds of pages in which to develop many characters.

We urge you to limit yourself to telling one person's story, at least when you are new to writing fiction or until you've studied several stories told from more than one perspective.

Third person limited: "He" or "she"

This is a wonderful point-of-view choice for a short story. Perhaps it's the best for most new writers, and it's certainly common for experienced writers, too. With third person you concentrate on one character, and you can go deeply, satisfyingly into that person's psyche or soul.

You have many choices when you use third person. You can limit yourself to observing what your character does and says and how others treat her: i.e., record only the externals of what happens. You can also, if you like, go into her mind revealing her thoughts and feelings and ways of seeing. You can even, if you want, pull way back and say things the character could never say or know about herself, reveal things about the situation that your main character doesn't know.

Here are some of your third-person point-of-view options:

- Record only the externals, what your main character does and says, how others treat him, and what happens. Check to see how some of Raymond Carver's, Ann Beattie's, and Ernest Hemingway's stories tend to rely heavily on the surface details.

- Add to the above what the character thinks and feels about the surface world. Read more of Flannery O'Connor to see how she adds these elements. The short story collections of Margaret Atwood, John Cheever, Alice Munro, and Theodore Weesner contain good models too.

- Stay entirely in a character's head showing the world as he perceives, smells, touches, hears, and tastes it. (Here your camera, using its mind-reading microphone, is right behind the character's eyeballs, recording only what he sees, thinks, and feels.) A good example of this is Jane Smiley's story, "Lily."

• Pull back from time to time and say things about a character he could never admit, perhaps never even know about himself or his situation. Again O'Connor does this often and so deftly we scarcely realize she has commented. So does Mark Helprin.

Note: you can do all of the above.

Use common sense when you think of point of view. Establish first what interests *you* about your character. If you have a character with a convoluted way of thinking and making sense (or not making sense) of her world or a character with a past that haunts her, you'll probably want to get into that character's head and explore how she thinks, feels, sees, and/or misperceives her world. You may even want to say a few things about the character she wouldn't know about herself. In that case you'll likely consider third-person point of view and want to use a camera in the way O'Connor does. If you think your main character will be satisfyingly revealed as you observe what she does and says, then perhaps, though not necessarily, your camera won't delve for long, perhaps not at all into her head, but rather record the surface events in such a way that readers will see beneath the surface to the deeper meanings.

First person: "I" or "we"

If you've ever acted in a play and felt yourself in the skin of another person, you'll know how interesting it can be to write in the first person. With first person, you become another character, thinking, feeling, remembering, seeing, touching, tasting, hearing, smelling, and above all reacting as your character does.

There's an immediacy to first person that appeals to many writers. Readers love to see how a first-person character makes sense of or fails to make sense of his world. It's fascinating to see the machinery of a mind at work.

You can decide if your first-person narrator is trustworthy or not. For an untrustworthy first person with a bizarre and very funny way of thinking, try Truman Capote's short story, "My Side of the Matter." Albert Camus, in his novella, *The Stranger*, has a narrator who disturbs us. When the story opens, the narrator's mother has just died and someone at work tells the narrator that he's sorry. The narrator doesn't understand why the man is sorry: after all, it's not *his* fault the mother died. Immediately we know something is wrong.

Mark Helprin gives us a reliable narrator in "Tamar." This narrator tells us of his involvement in a plan, in pre-World-War-II Europe, to smuggle art from Germany. The art was sold in England, and the profit was sent to help Jews escape from Germany. After telling us this, the narrator focuses on a specific experience he had one evening. The narrator, as he looks back, comments on his own past behavior.

This business of a narrator commenting *now* on an experience that happened earlier can make a story rich. We discussed on this effect in the guide "Choosing the Past or Present Tense." Some narrators appear to have just minutes ago had an experience they need to tell, and their comments are often less detached and elaborate than those of a narrator who's had years to reflect on something. A narrator who tells a story in the present tense ("I go down the street and, just ahead, see a dog") will likely have less objectivity still. Interestingly the last two paragraphs of Helprin's "Tamar" read almost like an essay. First-person narrators can comment in short passages or at length and not damage the reader's participation in their stories. We like to hear a narrator comment because how he makes sense of his world is part of the tension of the story. Alice McDermott in her short novel, *That Night*, and Alice Munro, in "Friend of My Youth," from the collection by that same title, have wonderful characters, tension, and drama, and narrators who comment often and with wisdom. (If you are writing in the third person ["He" or "She"], and you insert long essay-like statements, the reader may feel you are intruding, think you are being heavy-handed, and the magic spell of being "in a story" may be broken.)

A disadvantage of "I", and a serious one, is this: You, the writer, can't step in and say things about the character that she might not admit to or know about herself, can't include information or scenes that the narrator doesn't know about or see. This limits you. Again, there are exceptions that are important to know about. Ursula Hegi in *Floating in My Mother's Palm*, and Marilynne Robinson in *Housekeeping*, have each written connecting stories that, combined, are novels; each writer has a first-person narrator who tells the story and who gets into the minds of other characters, thus escaping the narrow first-person point of view.

This is how they do it. The first-person narrator ("I") starts telling of another character and usually tells some of the facts that the narrator knows. For instance, the narrator might say, "Harry lived two blocks from me when I grew up, and I knew this and that about Harry. One Saturday morning at eight o'clock, I saw him walk down main street with a big cardboard suitcase." Then the narrator will slip gradually into Harry's head in one of many ways such as this: "I can imagine what Harry thought as he walked down that street. The street was still wet after a long thunderstorm the night before and . . . ," etc. Or that narrator might say something like, "Perhaps he was thinking about . . ." and readers would learn his thoughts. At this point the narrator has slipped into telling Harry's story and can show things that she could never possibly know about Harry. First-person narrators who get into other characters' heads often use expressions like, "I can picture him," or "Probably he was thinking this," or "He must have felt," or "Surely he noticed," or "He must have known," or "decided," or "wondered." These phrases and others you'll invent will ease you from first person into third, where you can stay as long as you like—a few lines or many pages—(saying "he" saw or did or thought this or that) and from where you can glide back to the first-person ("I") narrator with ease and agility, not jarring your reader from belief and involvement. Going from first to third person is a kind of seduction you play with the reader.

Some stories are told from the point of view of a group of people such as students in one classroom, a family, people in a small town. In these stories, the writers say "we" did or said this and that, "we" believed this and saw that. A good example of this technique can be found in William Faulkner's short story, "A Rose for Emily."

Second Person: "You"

Sometimes writers like to address the readers with little asides that make readers feel they're included, even intimate or friendly with the writer. For instance, "You know people like that. You've seen them in small towns from coast to coast." Then the writer follows along after his main character.

Sometimes the "you" is used to get a reader on the writer's side or on the side of a first-person narrator. Let's say you're writing the story of a character who wants to appeal to the reader, to make the reader feel she's innocent of the murder she's been accused of. Your first-person narrator might say, "I know you've read of the murder in the *Herald*, know you must be convinced by the evidence against me, but you need to hear *my* story, these facts."

A writer or a first-person narrator can accuse or warn the reader: "You think you're safe, immune from catastrophe, but let me tell you something."

Some writers tell a whole story referring to their characters as "you"; for example, "You get in your car, drive down 8th Avenue, careful you don't hit the old drunk lurching across the corner of 8th and Sewall. You think you'll be on time, but the church bells chime and you realize you're already late." Writer Lori Moore uses second person in some of her stories in *Self-Help*. Jay McInerney uses second person in *Bright Lights, Big City*.

Using "you" can be dangerous when it appears sporadically. It can interrupt the readers' belief in and experience of the story, can take readers away from what's happening on the page and make them aware of themselves. A good guide for most stories is this: do nothing to interrupt the reader's immersion in your story. Exceptions abound.

Third Person Plural: "They"

Some writers want to tell the story of a group of people. Others tell of a group but zoom in on one or two characters within the group from time to time. Mark Helprin does the latter in an extraordinary story, "White Gardens" in his collection *Ellis Island and Other Stories*. There we are told about the funeral of some firemen. Throughout the story Helprin tells what happened in the church referring to the people there as "they," but he goes into the minds of two characters occasionally: the priest and one of the widows.

The danger in this kind of story is that readers usually find it easier to engage deeply, to enter the writer's world as participants if they can know one character and see the world through her eyes.

Final reminders

- Whatever point of view you choose, be logical, be clear, be consistent. And be considerate of your readers. They know nothing as they start your story. They need to feel secure, need to understand your ground rules, and need to know what's going on. Let them know who is telling your story, who your main character is, and where you stand in relation to your main character—i.e., whether your camera is up close, far away, or whether or not you'll be using a roving camera.

  Play fair with the reader. Don't start your story with a first-person narrator and on page ten leap without justification or preparation into the third person, or readers will be baffled. Don't promise your reader that this is a story about Sylvia and switch on page eight to Jack's story.

- Choose a point of view that is close enough to your experience so that you can write with good details and authority.

- Remember to respect *your* temperament and enthusiasm as you choose point of view.

📧 Exercises

1. Take a story you've written in, say, third person, and write it (or a few pages of it) in first. This will give you a good idea of the strengths and limitations of different perspectives.

2. Take one of your stories and write a few pages of it from another character's point of view.

3. Think of a rupture—a permanent break or temporary set-back—that you've experienced with someone who's impor-tant to you. Write the story of that rupture from the other person's point of view. Try it in first person from his or her viewpoint. Try it in third person.

4. Try the Flannery O'Connor roving camera approach. Use a third-person point of view. Show your main character in an argument with someone. Know a lot about this person. The argument should be critically important to your main charac-ter. Show the setting and record some of the argument. From time to time move your camera into the main character's head and write about how he feels and what he thinks. Then pull way back, and you, the writer, tell us something about the character he couldn't admit out loud, perhaps something he doesn't quite recognize about himself. Then zoom in to a close-up and capture his facial expressions, show what he and the other person do and say. Then get the camera behind the main character's eyeballs and show the actual things he sees, smells, hears, tastes, and touches. Stay in his head as the fight continues and let us know how he regards what is happening. Continue with this moving camera approach. Finally, reread the first few pages of O'Connor's "Everything That Rises Must Converge" and you will learn even more about how to use your camera.

5. Try the approach Saul Bellow uses in "Leaving the Yel-low House" where he stands way back at the start of the story and delivers a vividly rendered two-page statement about the main character before zeroing in on the specific day when

she wrecks her car and the dramatic action begins. You'll remember from our guide "Controlling Time" how D. H. Lawrence does this in "The Rocking-horse Winner." In his opening, he tells us about the woman who had no luck. He is very specific about her lack of luck, about her need for money, and about how the house she lives in cries out for more money. Then he begins the specific story concerning her young son's attempt to win money, to win luck.

6. Write from the point of view of an untrustworthy narrator as does Truman Capote in "My Side of the Matter." Assume the persona of someone who is paranoid, stupid, manic, gloomy, self-absorbed, or who suffers some other affliction of the spirit. Become that person. Use the first person, "I." Place your character in a specific conflict, and let your readers know right away that your narrator is untrustworthy, has strange, perhaps bizarre ways of seeing and reacting.

WRITING ABOUT VIOLENCE; WRITING ABOUT SEX

Violence

IN STORIES WHERE VIOLENCE OCCURS, YOU DON'T WANT TO BE sensational, but you don't want to avoid a tough, essential scene either. Pay attention to the meaning of the violent act. Pay attention to what leads up to it and/or what happens as a result of it. Work with the reverberations.

Be aware of the impression of violence that your main character receives. How does your main character feel, think, and act during the violent scene? Attitudes and behaviors in the midst of violence tell us a lot about people.

When you write a violent scene, create a dominant impression. You can't record each blow, although a few specific blows are usually essential. They'll make the scene believable and vivid.

Alice McDermott describes a street fight in her short novel, *That Night*. A gang of boys with chains and black jackets has appeared in the neighborhood to bring a girl, Sheryl, from her house. Sheryl's mother, crouched on the lawn by her house steps, tells them that Sheryl isn't there. The fathers and husbands, with baseball bats and snow shovels, fight the boys. The account is told by a first-person narrator who is an adult looking back on her childhood. McDermott sets the scene so that we see the place where the fight occurs. The narrator tells us a sprinkler was shooting weak sprays of water across the street. There was the sound of the collective gurgle of filters in backyard pools and "the odor of [the boys'] engines was like a gash across the ordinary summer air."

Then we see the violence—the impression of it and some well-chosen, specific blows—and we see a narrator interpreting the fight, making sense of it:

"Until then," McDermott writes, "I had thought all violence was swift and surefooted, somehow sleek, even elegant. I was surprised to see how poor it really was, how laborious and hulking." The narrator sees a man " . . . bend under the blow of what seemed a slow-moving chain, and then, just as gracelessly, swing his son's baseball bat into a teenager's ear." She watches people jumping on each other " . . . like obese, short-legged children, sliding and falling, raising chains that seemed to crumble backward onto their shoulders, moving bats and hoes and wide rakes that seemed as unwieldly as trees."

Notice that McDermott breaks down a stereotype of violence. She sees fighting in an original way.

Reread the John Yount passage we quoted on page 101 about the boy who jumps into a swimming hole and finds it full of cottonmouth water moccasins. Notice how we get the impression of many snakes in that scene and how we also see the one snake striking the boy's cheek again and again. Notice how we are told about the reaction of the other boys at the swimming hole as well as of the townspeople who can't forget what happened.

Here is how Faulkner shows a fight between two people in "Barn Burning." One boy hears someone accuse his father of being a barn burner and leaps at the accuser. The scene is told from the boy's point of view:

> Again he [the boy] could not see, whirling; there was a face in a red haze, moonlike, bigger than the full moon, the owner of it half again his size, he leaping in the red haze toward the face, feeling no blow, feeling no shock when his head struck the earth, scrabbling up and leaping again, feeling no blow this time either and tasting no blood, scrabbling up to see the other boy in full flight and himself already leaping into pursuit as his father's hand jerked him back, the harsh, cold voice speaking above him:"Go get in the wagon."

We get the impression of the fight as the boy experienced it. Interestingly we don't see any one blow as we do in most violent scenes.

Some writers avoid violent scenes altogether. In "María Concepción" by Katherine Anne Porter, Maria murders a woman she has caught with her husband. We don't need this scene because earlier, we've seen Maria cut the throats of chickens; she does this like a professional: efficiently, and without heat or hesitation. When Porter tells us that Maria goes after her husband's lover with a knife, our interest is not in how she kills the lover, but how she and her husband will feel and act after the murder.

Many people have been brought up to talk out differences rather than to fight them out, and so they may avoid violence in a story. Remember, though, that violence happens. Don't shrink from a fight scene when it is essential.

A warning: don't be melodramatic. Don't give into a temptation to use overblown language such as, "He drew back his arm, and thrust it forward with terrific force where his hard, white-knuckled fist dove into the nose of his adversary causing great spurts of blood to gush . . . ," etc. Instead, show the precise things that produced the violence: use specific details to create a dominant impression of the fight.

Exercises

1. If you've had a physical fight or seen one, write about it from your point of view. Get into your mind as you felt then and give an impression of the fight. Or describe the fight as an adult looking back, as do the narrators in McDermott's novel, *That Night* and John Cheever's story, "Goodbye, My Brother."

2. Think of someone you can't stand. Exaggerate that person's maddening qualities and your anger. Think of a situation where you could be arguing with him or her and where you know you'd be tempted to push the person into the water or off a porch or punch or slap him or her. Write about it, specifically, and push, punch, slap, or throw something. Or have the other person punch first.

There are some stories that need a dramatic fight scene. There are others made dramatic by the threat of one. A student writer wrote a moving coming-of-age story about a boy going bird hunting with his father and uncle. The uncle was drinking too much, getting belligerent. The boy's father, a controlled, mature man, decided it was time to go home. On the way to the car, they met some young men who had been smoking pot and were shooting rifles, aiming them straight up in the air. The uncle shouted at the young men, telling them how stupidly and dangerously they were behaving. The men and the uncle walked toward each other, gesturing, yelling louder. The boy's father very skillfully stopped the fight, and readers sensed the boy learning how to keep violence in check, coming to manhood.

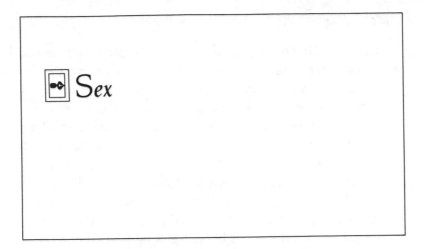

Sex

LOVE AND SEX FASCINATE MOST OF US. THEY'RE PART OF OUR lives and, therefore, part of our fiction. We know that how people make love reveals them and their relationships. Most of us don't want to write sensational or pornographic scenes. If we write an entire sex scene using one detail after another, we'll create the impression of a sex manual which is clinically detached. We want to suggest without being coy.

Many writers will show characters who are about to make love and stop there. Some writers will show the characters touching each other, perhaps starting to undress and then the writers will go on to the next scene. If we know a lot about a relationship, we'll have a good idea about the quality of love-making. Some writers will give an impression of the nature of the love-making by including just a few details.

A writer may want to let readers know the love-making took a long time, or was over in a few minutes. What people do immediately after making love reveals them. Do they remain close together? Do they talk? Does one partner fall immediately asleep while the other gets up and reads the funnies in the living room?

Pay attention to how you feel about writing love scenes. Don't force a love scene that makes you uncomfortable. On the other hand, remember that love-making can be the barometer of two people's feelings about each other and that a few well-chosen details can reveal a great deal.

In the first chapter of Louise Erdrich's *Love Medicine*, June and Andy, strangers, make love in the front seat of a car. Erdrich sets the scene with good details: the snow outside reflecting the light, the blast of heat when his hand accidentally knocks the controls, the smooth plastic seat, the "stretch fabric" of her slacks "that crackled with electricity and shed blue sparks when he pushed them down around her ankles." Erdrich reveals a lot about the characters and their relationship when Andy calls out another woman's name, when he falls quickly and heavily asleep, when June reacts first by trying to rouse him, then by staying quiet "until she felt herself getting frail again."

In "Yellow Woman" Leslie Marmon Silko sets her love scenes outdoors, making readers aware of the natural environment and its importance to her characters. The story begins lyrically: "My thigh clung to his with dampness, and I watched the sun rising up through the tamaracks and willows." Later she writes: "I felt him all around me, pushing me down into the white river sand." Both Silko and Erdrich write honestly but not graphically about love making. No clichés—just simple descriptions of the lovers, their thoughts, and the setting in which the love-making takes place.

Characters' perceptions of their love-making reveal them. If your characters are distinct and well-developed, their particular ways of seeing and behaving and understanding will carry over into their love-making just as they would into any other scene.

Beware clichés: pounding hearts, heaving breasts, hot breaths—any phrase that you've read before. Beware sentiment. Because falling in love and love-making are powerful events in our lives, some writers slip into gushy prose, such as: "Oh, the taste of her perfect lips upon mine as the night's stars twinkled down upon us." Sentiment and cliché are closely related.

Don't gush. Readers will groan with embarrassment.

Exercises

1. Try to recall love scenes from stories or novels that seemed particularly powerful. Reread the scenes. How much of the

love-making is spelled out for you? How much do you fill in with your own imagination?

2. Choose two of your characters who have a sexual relationship—even if you haven't included a love scene between them in a story. Write a short love scene. Write it three ways: objectively (looking on from the outside), then from the perspective of one partner, then from the perspective of the other. If you know these characters well, if you know how they've behaved in other situations, you must have some idea how they would make love. As you write, though, be open to surprises, to learning something new about these characters and their relationship.

FINDING MEANING

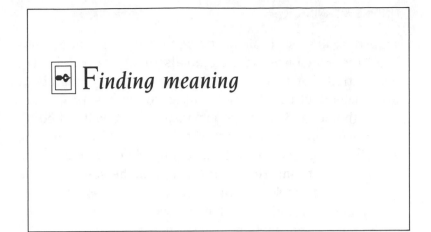

Finding meaning

SOME WRITERS FEEL UNCOMFORTABLE WHEN PEOPLE DISCUSS meaning or theme in their fiction. They say readers should appreciate a story for what it is and not dissect it. But a good story does have meaning. If we write merely about events without deeper reverberations, our stories will be shallow. It's a matter of significance. For example, making grape jelly may or may not be significant for you, depending on why you're making it. Maybe the process reminds you of someone you loved or a time in your life you'd like to remember or understand. Or maybe you're concentrating on making jelly in order to forget something painful. Just making grape jelly in order to make grape jelly is not a story—but what is revealed or comes to be understood through the process of making grape jelly could be.

Novelist Ted Weesner has said theme is "what the hell a story is really about."

Here's what we mean by theme. In Lawrence Sargeant Hall's short story, "The Ledge," the surface story is this: A man takes his son and nephew in a boat on the ocean to shoot ducks at the ledges. His skiff drifts away from the ledge. The tide comes in. They drown. Were the story told this way with only a few details about the ocean, the ledge, the man, and two boys, we'd have to say it was too bad they drowned, but really, so what? What's the point? By point we don't mean a moral lesson such as they should have seen their boat was tied securely, or those who take careless risks pay a price. We warned against such simplistic writing in our guide "End-ings." These are finger-wagging morals, the "be careful" kind of admonition that may be useful when you're learning about water safety but not in fiction, unless you're Aesop.

The theme in "The Ledge" is part of the story. It is tied up with the fisherman's character. The fisherman is a harsh man, and his wife has wondered occasionally what it would be like to live without him. Yet before he dies, as he stands on the ledge holding his son on his shoulders, he rises above his own limitations, and we see him as loving, tender, and noble. In the final scene where he lies stretched out, frozen on the dock, the wife sees him "absolved of his mortality." So the theme emerges through the character of the fisherman and what happens to him; we come to understand that a person can rise above himself, transcend limitations, and be forgiven.

Some writers say they know or sense their themes before they write. As we have said earlier, many writers feel this is dangerous, because it may lead them to push their characters around in order to fit their preconceived notions, resulting in stiff, flat characters. A way to avoid such temptation is to focus on a character who's in trouble. Slowly, as you write and revise, look as deeply as you can into character, letting the theme reveal itself to you.

If the meaning of your story has eluded you after a draft or two, go back to the first line and explore your character deeply; if you explore her deepest yearnings, frustrations, needs, and drives, you can't escape theme.

Theme can't be a revelation in the last few lines—that's a contrived, tacked-on ending. Theme begins with line one and, like conflict, builds. Think of how theme works in music. We hear it in the first notes and it is repeated, extended, altered, enriched all through. In stories theme operates in every detail, every moment. All through "The Ledge," we see the harshness of the fisherman, and his limitations as well as some of his good qualities, which, as he dies, will prevail.

Here's another example of theme. In Joyce's "Eveline," which we have previously discussed, the main character must decide whether or not to leave her father and Ireland for a new life in a new land. She sits by a window, reviewing her options. Although she sees exquisitely the problems of her life in town, the town is at least familiar. She decides not to leave. So what? The "so what," or theme, involves fear of the unfamiliar and the terrible hold even bad situations can have on people too fearful to take risks.

Don't worry about theme until you've finished a first draft. After that first draft, look for the theme or themes that seem to be emerging—even slightly—in your details. Look for thematic clues in your main character. Strong passages or moments in a story often contain thematic statements. Once you've found your theme, you can add details that enhance it and eliminate details that don't. You can stretch thematically important scenes and cut scenes that lead us away from theme. You can shape your story to reflect your own growing understanding of what's important, of what the hell your story is really about.

By the final draft, you should be able to justify everything that's in the story. Not that you should go through and say, "This is here because . . . ," but, even though in a first or second or third draft you weren't sure why this moment or detail was included, by the time you're done with a story, each word should contribute to meaning, and you should have a sense of rightness about your decisions.

A story is a unified work of art. Like other works of art, it has purpose and meaning. In the end, every component must convey that meaning or be cut. Sensitive attention to a developing theme can help you pull a story together without forcing it into a preconceived mold.

⊶ Exercises

1. Read several of your favorite published stories. Ask yourself what is the theme in each. Notice how it operates throughout; notice words, phrases, images, commentary, and actions that contribute directly to theme. If you have trouble identifying the theme, ask a friend or two what they think the story is really about.

2. Review one of your stories that seems to lack theme. Where are the strongest, most vivid passages? What do these passages have in common with each other? These commonalities suggest theme—the thread of meaning, however slight, which begins to connect them. Look for thematic clues in your main character and ask yourself if you need to explore her more fully.

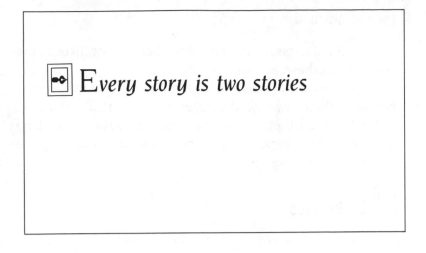

Every story is two stories

GRACE PALEY SAID, "I KNOW I HAVE A STORY WHEN I HAVE TWO stories." Two stories make one when strong story lines and themes intersect. Each enhances the other, creating reverberations.

For example, you begin writing about a fight between neighbors and in the writing discover that your point-of-view character is also quite ill. Then you're writing about two fights: a neighborhood dispute and a fight for health and life. Perhaps both fights disturb your main character's peace of mind. One fight reflects and deepens the other. The neighborhood dispute takes on more significance because the reader knows about the character's personal problems, the health anxieties are dramatized, perhaps indirectly, when neighbor confronts neighbor, when the shouting begins, when the fist fight erupts. You know you have a story because you have two stories. Your story contains an automatic parallel or conflict.

Rebecca Rule's story "The Man Who Saw Bigfoot" is about a man named Sam Crawford, who saw a strange creature while out hunting. That's the surface story: the sighting and its repercussions. The second story emerged when Rule realized that Sam, like bigfoot, had suffered greatly in his life, and was suffering still from old wounds. In a way his suffering allowed him to see bigfoot. One story concerned an amazing turn in a man's life: bigfoot in the apple orchard. The second concerned how a man, how anyone, copes over a lifetime with personal tragedy. "The Man Who Saw Bigfoot" lives at the point where these two stories intersect.

Often writers will begin with one story, then push, probe, and draft their way into the second. What's really going on here? they'll ask themselves. The trick is always to be looking for that second deeper story, to be ready for it and receptive when it whispers to you.

Exercises

1. Read Grace Paley's "A Conversation With My Father" or some other short, dense story by a fine writer. List the stories that make up the story. In Paley, there's the story of an argument between a woman and her father, the story of a writer's relationship with her art, the story of a daughter trying to deal with the imminent death of her father, and several others. Test the depth of the story by separating out the stories.

2. Go through a draft of one of your own pieces looking for the second, third, and fourth stories. This is the story of _____ and the story of _____ and the story of _____. If you find only one story, look for hints or openings for further development—and develop them.

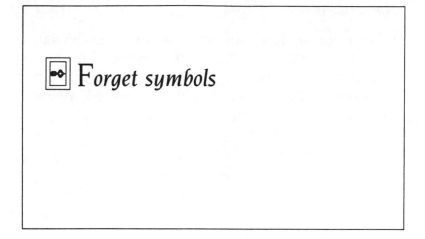

Forget symbols

LEAVE THE SUBJECT OF SYMBOLS TO LITERATURE CLASSES. A concern for symbols that are laden with meaning can kill your story. This is why: we should write to find out the truth of our characters' lives, to describe things as clearly as we can. If we're concerned with our main character's crooked teeth as symbolic of his economically poor background, our attention will be on symbols rather than on our real job of describing the precise angle of those teeth, of making this set of crooked teeth unlike any other set in the world. Our prose will stink of "I Found A Symbol!"; our readers won't see those teeth as distinctive, won't believe the teeth exist, and therefore our would-be symbol will collapse.

Concern for symbols is for readers after the hard work of writing has been done. It is something discovered in a story long after the writer is busy writing something else. We don't mean to dismiss the concern for symbols in literature courses. But if you are writing and think you have a great symbol here, you're not concentrating on your major task. Tell yourself to stop it. Concentrate on describing each person and object exactly, on being honest, on seeing deeply into the heart of your main character, on finding out what happens next, on using the right words. That's enough to keep any writer busy.

Exercise

If you find it impossible not to be aware of symbols as you write, find some of them in a published story you love. Then study the specific details, the words, and the sentences that produced the symbols. You'll appreciate that the writer had to be concentrating on what he or she was trying to say, on the actual words, rather than on the abstract idea of a symbol.

REVISING, EDITING, PUNCTUATING, AND PUBLISHING

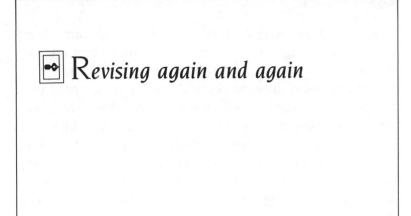

Revising *again and again*

REVISION MEANS STEPPING BACK FROM YOUR STORY, RESEEING what you've done, and then going back again to improve it. Revision can mean giving up your preconceptions, surrendering yourself to the words on the page and to the truth on the page, or it can mean throwing out the whole story and starting over. Revision usually means trying to know your characters more deeply and fully, working for more insight. It means looking for solutions, taking risks. You may write pages of dialogue just to see what characters have to say, then cut 95 percent of that dialogue. You may realize you haven't gone deeply enough into your character and add a five-page flashback. Or you may turn the story in a new direction just to see what happens, then backtrack to the original story line. Revision can mean changing your main character's age from twenty-five to eighteen or writing from a different point of view. It can mean writing scenes, refining scenes, expanding them, rearranging or deleting them. It may mean writing ten different beginnings or endings. Revision means unifying your story, making it a work of art, making each part contribute to the whole. It means making tough choices. In our section on revision, page 38 in the guide "Writers at Work," we stress how often professional writers revise.

Editing or fine-tuning is part of revision, but revision is more than editing. Revision means seeing the big picture, looking at your story through the eyes of readers, understanding what is there on the page and what is not.

Writers often revise as they write their first drafts. Many write the first page on day one, then return to that page on day two, revise it, and write the second page. On day three, they revise pages one and two and write a third. By the time they've reached page fifteen, they've revised their lead fifteen times. A few writers say certain stories require very little revision, but this is as rare, we think, as giving birth without pain.

Each revision, each change large or small, sets up a reverberation within your story, mandating more changes. As the story nears completion the revisions become more precise and contained: you become a tinkerer—and the tinkering can fascinate you when you're at work on a story you believe in.

Below are some questions that may help you think about your drafts, immerse yourself in them, and guide you through revision. Certainly you would never test your story with each item on our list, but we hope the questions show you some of the points writers consider as they revise.

REVISOR'S CHECKLIST

1. *Is this a story?*
   Does something happen?
   Is a new way of seeing something or someone revealed?
   Is there a sense at the end of life not being the same
      anymore?

2. *Conflict*
   What is the conflict?
   Is the conflict creating tension all the way through?
   Does it erupt in a crisis or is there a moment of revelation?

3. *Meaning*
   What does this story mean?
   Is the meaning built throughout the story or is it a
      last-minute revelation?
   Does each section of the story contribute to meaning?
   Does each detail, each line of dialogue, each word
      contribute to meaning?
   Does the story veer in a false direction?

Is this false direction more interesting than the rest
of the story? If so, you may find that the false direction
may be, in fact, the true one.

4. Ending

Does the ending reverberate with meaning and
resolution?

Does the ending grow out of everything that's gone on in the
story or is it tacked on, unjustified?

Do you overshoot the ending by explaining too much or going
on to an unnecessary scene or scenes? Should you cut the
last line or paragraph?

5. Character

Do you focus on a character in trouble—internal or external
or both?

Is your main character rich and complex?

Do you reveal character deeply, with moments of insight
all through?

6. Point of View

Have you chosen the best point of view for your story?

Is the point-of-view character the one most changed?

7. Beginning

Do you start with conflict or tension in the first paragraph?

Does the lead pull the reader into the heart of the story?

Does the lead give the reader essential information?

Do you begin your story too soon? That is, do you
diddle around for a few paragraphs?

8. Tense

Does the primary action take place in the present or past?

Is this choice of tense appropriate?

Have you been consistent and clear in your use of tense?

9. Honesty

Is the story honest or does it rely on a
gimmicky plot, flat characters, words that are not exact,
and an unbelievable last-minute resolution or trick ending?

*Are you writing to explore the truth of a character's
life? If you're writing to prove a point or show that a
character behaves in such and such a way, stop writing.
You're pushing your character around and he will be stiff.
Start again and write to see what that character will do when
you don't force him.*

10. Clarity

    Is the story clear?

    Do readers know who's who and what's at stake?

    *Do you need, from time to time, to deliver essential information
    in a straightforward way?*

11. Structure

    *Is the story paced well? Does it move along too fast or too
    sluggishly?*

    Does each scene earn the space it occupies?

    *Could some scenes or parts of scenes be cut back or eliminated
    because the information isn't that significant or is repeated
    elsewhere?*

    Are there parts that need to be filled out?

    Are there any missed opportunities?

    *Do the flashbacks and background information add to your
    main character's burden and push the story ahead?*

    *Does the story move along briskly or are there
    sluggish, boring passages?*

12. Language

    Is the language honest, exact?

    *Does it create an experience for the reader with
    sensuous details; i.e., can the reader see, hear, taste,
    touch, and smell?*

Exercise

Look at one of your stories after reading this checklist. See if
you can locate a central flaw in the story. Work to fix that. Then
work, section by section, to revise in other ways suggested by
the checklist.

Some writers let stories cool for several days or weeks before they revise. They use the time away to gain distance and detachment so they can see their stories clearly. Others don't put stories away; they stay with them, revising again and again. Try different methods to see what works for you.

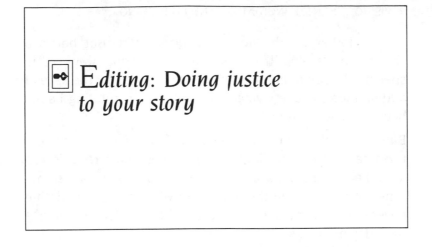

Editing: Doing justice to your story

IN THE PREVIOUS CHAPTER WE FOCUSED ON MAJOR REVISION, issues of meaning, character, structure, and so forth. Where this kind of major revision ends and the nitpick editing begins, who can say? Certainly there is overlap.

You've had teachers urge you to edit: to be specific and accurate, to cut unnecessary words, clichés, sentiment, exaggerations, melodrama. Probably those teachers were patient. We're going to be blunt: poor editing and sloppy sentences will ruin your story. Its strengths will be obscured. If your sentences are filled with clichés, melodrama, and purple prose, you will appear ignorant, even stupid. Readers will be embarrassed for you.

You must not do this to yourself or your fiction. If you were at a dinner party with a friend who was telling a wonderful story, but who burped loudly during each sentence he spoke, you'd get him aside later and have a little talk with him.

Here's our little talk about careful editing.

Be specific

Develop the habit of being specific. Be generous with details. Take advantage of opportunities to give the reader more information.

Not: Carlotta's roommate was beginning to develop some extremely irritating habits such as leaving her clothes on the floor.

The clothes on the floor is a good start. But here's a chance to develop the roommate's irritating ways more specifically. You're not heaping on details just for the sake of adding more. You're giving examples of her irritating habits because they matter.

But: Carlotta's roommate began to leave her clothes and pizza cartons on the floor and play her blues records too loud. Each night she would talk for an hour, then two, sometimes three hours on the telephone with her boyfriend. She never washed her dishes anymore or helped clean the house Saturday mornings.

Edit for detail. Remember to rely on the five senses, especially sight. Ask yourself: can readers see?

Be accurate

Not: The low bushes . . .
But: The scraggly low junipers.

Not: She nearly fainted when she saw the worm in her salad.
But: She flinched . . .

Use strong verbs

Not: The girls were running around under the basket in apparent confusion, red uniforms swarming blue.
But: The girls tangled under the basket, red uniforms swarming blue.

When you use precise, active verbs the reader gets a vivid picture. If you have a choice, write in the active voice rather than the passive.

Not Passive: Claude was kissed by Ann.
But Active: Ann kissed Claude.

In the passive voice the object of the verb (Claude, the one who gets kissed) becomes the subject of the sentence— a backwards way of presenting information. Passive constructions are usually longer than active, less direct, and less effective; readers engage passively in your prose. Active constructions emphasize the action; readers engage actively in your prose.

If possible, avoid "ing" constructions, which slow the pace of your sentences.

Not: I am going.
But: I go.

Not: She will be going.
But: She will go.

Not: He was going.
But: He went.

Cut unnecessary words

Unneeded words clutter a sentence and distract readers. A beginning tennis player may wave his racket at absurd angles when serving, leap at the wrong time to swat the ball, bang his knee with the racket. He looks ridiculous. The ball hits the net. A professional wastes no motion. Each movement has purpose. The result is power and beauty. The same is true of prose.

Not: This was going to be such an exciting, unique day! Roland awoke that morning with the knowledge that he was going to take the trip east—the big one—for the very first time in his life. He'd lived all his life in Kansas—flat country—and he'd never seen a large hill, much less a mountain. He was headed to the Northeast where he'd see and actually climb a mountain in the Northeast—Mount Washington!
But: Today Roland, who had never travelled outside Kansas, would fly to New Hampshire and climb Mt. Washington.

Cut clichés

All clichés, though they might have been clever when first coined, have been used so often they have lost their effectiveness. When you use a cliché, you lose authority as well as the reader's interest. Readers want a writer to see the world with clear eyes. They want originality. Clichés are hand-me-downs.

Often new writers don't recognize clichés. A general rule: if you've heard a phrase before, beware. Here are some examples of clichés that will clog your stories. If you find yourself writing one of these expressions, consider this an opportunity to cut the cliché out in revision and replace it with something stronger. Or maybe the sentence would be tighter and more powerful with no replacement.

achieved her goal; as a matter of fact; as soon as the opportunity presented itself; biding my time; blonde and blue-eyed; blood-curdling scream; breathtakingly beautiful; brown as a berry; butterflies in her stomach; carefree children; caved in under the pressure; cemented their friendship; chin up; codependency; couldn't take it any more; crabby old man; cute as a button; cute blonde; dark and stormy night; decisive victory; delusions of grandeur; devastatingly handsome; drinking and carousing; efficient German; evil glint in her eye; excitable Italian; eyes darted; eyes grew large (round) with surprise; face facts; first-name basis; frozen in his tracks; gentle breeze; grief stricken; hair stood on end; hard facts; head held high; high hopes; his heart stopped; horns of a dilemma; horror-struck; hostile relationship; it was heaven; it was hell; jaw dropped; last but not least; let me make a long story short; lightning fast; little old lady; majestic pines; mischievous grin; mutual admiration society; my heart melted; my heart pounded; never lost courage (faith); open and honest; overcame his handicap; packed and ready to go; partying till the wee small hours (cows come home); peace and serenity; pleased as punch; pulled himself together; pushed it to the back of her mind; raced through my mind; tranquil lake; rustic bridge (cabin, village); sank back on the pillow; shivers went up his spine; slept like a baby; slipped out; soft as a kitten; sparkling eyes; spirited horse; stiff with fear; sun-drenched room; sun filtered through the curtains; sweet as pie; tall, dark, and handsome; tender age; time of your life; tranquil lake (scene); twinkling blue eyes; warm, open relationship; went through hell; when you stop and think about it; wide-eyed innocence; wind-whipped branches; won hands down; young and carefree

Getting rid of clichés is so important, you might go through a draft with just that in mind—a cliché purge. If you do use a cliché, know why you're using it, and be certain that it will have the impact you want on the reader.

A few writers deliberately work with clichés, trying to find fresh meaning in old words. But these are writers whom readers trust because all through the stories the words have been exact. When the cliché is used, it is used in a fresh way and often delights the reader.

Some characters may think in clichéd ways. This can become an interesting flaw. Truman Capote's first person narrator uses clichés in "My Side of the Matter"; we know he can't see his world clearly, and therefore we don't trust him. If one of your characters uses clichés, be sure the reader knows it is the character's way of seeing, not yours. For example: "Her father had told her the early bird catches the worm, and, if she wanted to make something of her life she'd have to be that bird—out alone in the damp, out ahead of the rest." This is the father, not the writer relying on a cliché.

Cut clunkers

A clunker is a do-nothing phrase that lacks specific information and purpose. It does nothing to push your story ahead. Clunkers include empty phrases—there is, it seemed that, at this point in time, due to the fact that—phrases with no color, no imagery, little meaning. They lengthen your sentences without adding a thing. Any redundant expression is also a clunker: The reason was because; great big huge; it's location was fifty-fourth street; tuna fish; scrawny weakling; at 7:00 pm that evening.

Whatever you say in your stories: say it short, say it right, say it once, and move on.

Avoid sentimental interpretations of powerful events

Writers should not avoid powerful emotions, but they should avoid turning a strong emotion into a sentimental one. At potentially sentimental, mushy moments in your prose—a funeral, a love scene, a farewell, a child's birthday party—go on the alert. Trust that this moment is strong in itself and that you don't need to heap on sentiment with adjectives and clichés. Show exactly what happens—the facts, the details— and trust them to evoke a response in the reader. Readers don't respond to trite representations of emotional moments: the tear rolling down the mourner's face; the lover's pounding heart; the balloons, ice cream, cake, and candles at the birth-day party. Instead readers will be moved by unusual details, the ones that make the funeral or love scene or birthday party distinctive. Maybe at the grave someone's beeper goes off or the minister drops the Bible or a firetruck roars past. Maybe as the couple kisses, his breath smells of licorice or garlic. Maybe at the party the child gets the hiccups or falls down the stairs and sprains an ankle.

In life each burial, each love scene, each party is like no other. It is our business to reflect these distinctions in our stories.

Avoid arty expressions

Some writers, moved by a beautiful lake at night, strain to be poetic, and the result can embarrass readers. The prose stinks of would-be art: clichés, too many adjectives, outra-geous exaggeration. Readers hear violins quivering in the background.

If you want to create a beautiful scene on the page, trust your material. If a scene is beautiful and you describe it accurately, the reader will see the beauty. If a comparison emerges naturally, and is fitting, keep it. But avoid trite ex-pressions, pompous phrases and cheesy alliteration. Don't let the reader smell your sweat.

Here's an example of a writer trying too hard. This is pur-ple prose:

> Ah, but how he loved to look back to that summer he was ten and when, barefooted and without a care in the world he would frolic innocently through the lush yet prickly green grass which tickled his toes and his vital ever-searching imagination to the little lake's uneven edge and there, there by the cooling, ever-blue waters, the gentle breezes blew blissfully against his youthful skin and whispered of nature's marvelous mysteries.

If you find yourself using words like majestic, myriad, stun-ning, achingly, perfect, or wondrous, calm yourself. Begin again. Imagine the scene. Write the actual things that you see, or that your character sees. Be accurate.

Avoid *exaggeration and melodrama*

Trust that your material is interesting and that you don't have to gussy it up. Trust that if you tell the reader that Manuel had never been west of the Mississippi and was going to Seattle for the first time this doesn't have to be garnished with "and he had never been so excited in his life!"

Writers who trust their material write in a simple, straightforward way. Amy Tan in *The Joy Luck Club* writes about the drowning of a child, from the perspective of his sister, without a trace of exaggeration or melodrama. The scene is all the more moving because of her restraint. Rose Hsu Jordan is supposed to be watching after her brother Bing on the family outing by the sea. She thinks her father is watching him, too, and so grows careless. There is excitement, distraction when the father hooks a fish. She sees Bing in the distance, on the edge of the reef, and realizes he may fall in. Then Tan writes: "And just as I think this, his feet are already in the air, in a moment of balance, before he splashes into the sea and disappears without leaving so much as a ripple in the water."

The reader sees what happens from the narrator's point of view, feels her shock and horror. The language is accurate. Had it been inflated, the power would have been lost.

Exercise

When you and your story are ready for a final draft, use this checklist.

FINAL NITPICK CHECKLIST

- Is each paragraph, sentence, and word necessary?
- Have you used strong, active verbs that engage readers?
- Have you used adjectives and adverbs sparingly and effectively?
- Have you varied the length of your sentences? Are your paragraphs too long or too short?
- Have you eliminated all clunkers, clichés, exaggerations, sentiment, and melodrama?

- When read aloud does the story flow?
- Are repetitions intentional, effective, and graceful?
- Does sentence rhythm reflect action and character, sensibility and meaning?
- Is the punctuation correct and does it enhance meaning? (See our guide on punctuation tips.)
- Have you misspelled any words?
- Is the story as complete and polished as you can make it?
- Is the type dark? (Eye-strain makes readers irritable.)
- Are the margins straight? (Presentation affects readers' impressions.)
- Is the story ready for readers?

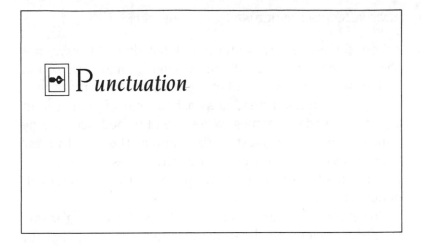

Punctuation

THINK OF PUNCTUATION AS A MEANS TO GUIDE YOUR READER. Think of punctuation as signs marking the streets of the city that is your story. Without these signs, the reader would become confused, even lost. With them, the reader travels with ease and confidence.

Fiction writers use sentence structure, rhythm, repetition, and punctuation to approximate the power of the spoken word, and to let readers know precisely what they mean.

Punctuation can change meaning. Note the difference between: "Please come in" and "Please, come in." The second version smacks of an order. Or: "Help Jack." "Help! Jack!" "Help, Jack." Same words; different meanings.

This guide includes punctuation tips that will help you say what you mean. You may be tempted, in your quest for clear communication, to invent new punctuation. Resist this temptation. Three exclamation points in a row don't make a statement stronger, they just look strange and pull your reader's attention away from the content of the story. Instead of being engaged by the characters and their problems, the reader will think about the writer who typed in those three exclamation points and wonder what might have possessed her to do such a thing.

Punctuation should not call attention to itself. It should simply tell us how to read a sentence. It should show us how ideas and images connect. The more you know about your choices for structure and punctuation, the better. In drafts, writers sometimes try sentences fifteen different ways, not changing the content at all, just changing shape and sound and punctuation to see what works best. Of course, each change—a comma instead of a dash, a semicolon instead of a period—shades meaning. Writers tend to be fascinated by punctuation, by the finest of fine tuning. They tend to ask themselves repeatedly, How can I structure these sentences so they mean what I want them to mean, so that a reader can understand what I understand.

Sometimes you must break rules. That's fine, as long as this pulls your readers into the story rather than confusing them or pushing them out.

The rules cited here just touch the complexities of punctuation. Don't rely on them alone. Buy a thorough grammar handbook. Many are available, including the widely used and highly respected *Chicago Manual of Style*. One of the most thorough is *The St. Martins Handbook* by Andrea Lunsford and Robert Connors. And, of course, there's the classic *Elements of Style* by Strunk and White.

When in doubt, look it up. A few careless errors can break a reader's concentration or cause an editor to reject a fine story.

Quotations " "

When characters speak, use quotation marks.

> "The best part of moving," she told Matthew, "besides your marvelous promotion, is getting a new doctor."

Notice that the comma appears *inside* the end quotation mark in the first part of the sentence. So does the period at the end.

Commas and periods always go inside the end quotation mark.

Question marks and exclamation points may go inside or outside. If the material quoted forms the question or exclamation, put the question mark or exclamation point inside the end quotation mark. If the material quoted is part of a greater question or exclamation, put the punctuation outside the quotation mark.

"What'll you do for two whole weeks?" he asked again last night.

How can I throw them away when my dying mother said, "I've saved these all for you"?

Notice that attribution ("he said," "she asked," "I whispered") breaks up the quotation.

Where you place the attribution determines the rhythm of the sentence. Repositioning attribution allows you to emphasize different words by changing the sentence rhythm.

"No," she says, "I mean it."
"No, I mean it," she says.
She says, "No, I mean it."

Or:

"My God!" Stacey leaned forward. "How long did the storm last?"
Stacey leaned forward. "My God. How long did the storm last?"

Do not use quotation marks for indirect quotations.

Indirect: Matthew told her he'd come swimming with her if she'd give him a minute to change.
Direct: "I'll come swimming with you, if you'll give me a minute to change," Matthew said.

Do not quote thoughts. Some writers do, but saving quotation marks for what is actually spoken avoids reader confusion: Did she think this or did she say it?

Her laugh is brittle, embarrassed. The sculpture looks suddenly crude. Randy could have done better.

Here, the sentence "Randy could have done better" is clearly a thought scooped from the mind of the main character. Even though the sentence sounds like something she might have said, the reader knows she didn't because there are no quotation marks.

On the other hand, if a line is quoted, the reader knows it was spoken aloud, even without "she said."

Her laugh is brittle, embarrassed. The sculpture looks suddenly crude. "Randy could have done better."

The author also could have written the following:

"Randy could have done better," she thought.

While this option avoids confusion, it creates a great distance between the reader and the character. (We address the issue of distance in our guide "Point of View.") The quotation marks put the reader on the outside looking in, instead of putting the reader directly in the character's mind.

Use single quotation marks to quote within a quote.

> "I asked you for a permit last winter," I said. "And you said, 'Oh Raymond, I couldn't do that. I don't believe in trapping helpless animals. It's cruel.'"

In quotations that run more than one paragraph, show the continuation by placing quotation marks at the beginning of each new paragraph, but save the closing quotation marks for the end of the last paragraph.

Writers sometimes break rules (or bend them) in order to get the *sound* right—to show, for example, how a character speaks. Notice the way the following sentence fragments show the character's surprise.

> "And his wife? She was there? Too?" Stacey said.

A more conventional sentence structure would create a different effect.

> "Was his wife there too?"

Use a comma, question mark, or exclamation point before attribution, but never double punctuate.

> *Not*: "Do you really believe that?", she asked.
> *But*: "Do you really believe that?" she asked.

Also, save periods for the end of the sentence. Never place a period before your attribution.

> *Not*: "Get out of there." I said.
> *Not*: "Get out of there.", I said.
> *But*: "Get out of there," I said.
> *Or*: "Get out of there!" I said.

Semicolon ;

Semicolons tell your reader that more material is coming and that material is equal in importance to what has come before.

"Hang on," a semicolon says, "we're not done yet." Semicolons clarify by breaking up (or joining) equal, related thoughts.

> My husband's hair is mostly white now; it hangs in sweet damp curls over the collar of his yellow slicker.

These two independent clauses could be written as separate sentences—that is, you could substitute a period and a capital letter for the semicolon. But by separating the one sentence into two, you'd lose the close relationship between the images.

> My husband's hair is mostly white now. It hangs in sweet damp curls over the collar of his yellow slicker.

Semicolons are also used to separate or join items in a series if the items are long or contain commas. In this case, the semicolon replaces the comma. It acts as a kind of super-comma, and it distinguishes major divisions from minor ones.

> I head to the poultry barn for the familiar and exotic: Wyandotte chickens as delicately marked as an impressionist painting; White Bali ducks with puffballs on their heads; whispering Muscovies, their faces red and fleshy; spirited geese in whose round eyes I read a challenge.

The semicolons distinguish four major divisions in the sentence—Wyandotte chickens, White Bali ducks, Muscovies, and geese. Within these divisions are subdivisions, indicated by comma breaks ("whispering Muscovies, their faces red and fleshy"). The semicolons tell us what goes with what, so the reader doesn't have to reread and regroup along the way.

Note: Type one space after a semicolon, just as you would after a comma; type two spaces after periods, question marks, exclamation points, and colons.

Colon :

A colon introduces material that explains, elaborates on, or illustrates what has come before. The semicolon connects equals; the colon subordinates.

When you're trying to decide whether to use a colon or semicolon ask yourself: does the second complete thought explain, elaborate on, or illustrate the first? If it does, choose the colon. Ask yourself: is the second complete thought separate, equal, but closely connected? If it is, use the semicolon.

In the following example, the second complete thought explains the first, so we choose a colon.

> He mentioned no specific transgressions, but Sharon knew exactly what he was talking about: Randy and his inflatable dragon, Puff, had drifted in front of the Dahl house.

In the following example, the two images are closely associated; we want to give them equal weight, so we choose the semicolon.

> The rim is an iron hoola-hoop; when the tree gyrates, I imagine, the hoop twirls at its gray waist.

You may capitalize the first letter of a complete thought following the colon or you may leave it lower case. Do not capitalize after a semicolon. Do not capitalize after a colon if a fragment or fragments follow, for example:

> The children made it tolerable: a home-made chemistry set, poster paints on four-foot-wide newsprint spread across the kitchen floor, a triangular tree house she'd made with them, rowing on the river, catching bass.

Because the pause after a colon is longer than after a comma, colons can emphasize startling or important material, for example:

> Remember what I said: Colons can be used for emphasis.

Dash —

A dash is a multi-purpose mark of punctuation usually indicating a significant shift in thought or the pattern of a sentence. It may be substituted for a colon, comma, or even the semicolon.

Resist the temptation to overuse the dash—too many on a page look like the scratching of chicken feet.

Use dashes in long sentences when you've already used up some other options: if, for example, you've already incorporated a colon and/or semicolon and a comma or two, but have more material to plug in.

My husband is easy to spot: he is the tallest figure on deck, and he stands where I stood in the stern—a good sign.

Dashes, like commas, tend to travel in pairs—one at the beginning of an interrupting element, one at the end. (Unless the sentence ends first, as it does in the previous example.) It's easy to forget the second dash, so watch for it.

My new love kicks black leaves away from the iron rim: the wood of the wagon wheel—spokes and frame—long since rotted or burned.

Below, a dash substitutes for a colon:

They are funny, chatty, joyful women—the kind Matthew calls typical Sharon friends.

Below, a dash substitutes for a comma:

I feel uneasy hearing that word in connection with the boat— as if one of us is missing the point.

A dash may be used in dialogue to show that the speaker was interrupted.

"If you really want to help—"
"I do," she said.

Note: Type the dash as two hyphens with no spaces on either side or between them. In printed text the dash appears as one solid line, slightly longer than a hyphen. Most word processors and typewriters don't have a dash key, so you must substitute two hyphens. Using one hyphen to indicate a dash will confuse readers.

Ellipsis . . .

An ellipsis consists of three dots with spaces between them and indicates that something has been left out. Academic and technical writers use the dots to show that not all of an expert's words have been included in the quoted material. In fiction, an ellipsis is most commonly used to show that a speaker has trailed off while speaking aloud.

"Well," he said slowly, "she did mention something about . . ."

237

Some writers use the three dots for the ellipsis and a fourth to end the sentence. Other writers might emphasize the trailing-off effect by using just three. Don't use five, six, or twenty dots to make the pause or trailing off more dramatic. This will just distract your readers.

Comma

The common advice, "If you hear a pause, insert a comma," does not always hold true. Many rules govern the use of commas, but the pauses you hear could represent anything from the need for a colon to a natural, rhythm break after a strong noun. Here are a few comma rules that are useful for fiction writers.

Use commas to separate items in a series or list.

Lists work well to present a lot of information concisely. They can help you furnish your fictional world. They can help you sketch a character quickly. They can help you juxtapose the serious and the silly, the significant and the insignificant. They can help you move quickly through time, or expand time with excruciating detail. For lists within lists, read Tim O'Brien's "The Things They Carried," which details the emotional lives of American soldiers in Vietnam through what they carried on their backs and in their hearts.

> As a first lieutenant and platoon leader, Jimmy Cross carried a compass, maps, code books, binoculars, and a .45-caliber pistol that weighed 2.9 pounds fully loaded.

You may choose to put a comma before the "and" that signals the last item in the series—or you may choose not to. In this case, and in every decision you make about punctuation, go with what sounds best, what looks good, what illustrates your meaning, and, especially, what is clear.

Use commas to set off words, phrases, or clauses that interrupt the flow of the sentence.

These are nonessential elements that we've italicized in the examples below. If you've used commas correctly to set off these interrupters, you'll be able to combine what comes before the first comma with what comes after the second into a complete, sensible sentence.

Sam couldn't spend more than an hour or two on a deer stand, *especially in cold weather*, before his bones began to ache.

The end of the clothesline, *half-pitched to a spoke at the corner of the garage*, is painted red.

In each case the base sentence makes sense without the italicized phrase. Some writers remember to put in the first comma—they hear the pause—but forget the second. In a complicated sentence, finding the base sentence will help you determine where the second comma belongs.

That book, *which belonged to my great-grandmother*, was nearly lost in the fire.

Note: *Which* introduces nonessential elements. *That* introduces essential ones, which is the difference between *which* and *that*. If, in the example above, the phrase "belonged to my great-grandmother" *identified* the book and so was essential to the sentence, the sentence might be written: "The book that belonged to my great-grandmother was nearly lost in the fire." Essential elements are not set off by commas.

In fiction we name the world. Sometimes in one sentence we will name someone or something twice. The second name is usually set off by commas.

My new love, Alan, pulls the hoop from the delicate grasp of white roots, grasses, and crawling ivies.

In this example "my new love" is another name for "Alan."

But he robbed her during the last seven months of Amy, her youngest daughter, the most imaginative.

In this example, two names follow the name Amy. She may also be called "her youngest daughter" or "the most imaginative," but these other names are not essential for the reader to understand the "who" of the sentence.

On the other hand, sometimes a second name is essential.

He had robbed her of her daughter Amy.

If she has more than one daughter, both the name "her daughter" and the name "Amy" must be included to distinguish this daughter from, say, her other daughters, Denise and

Claire. An essential name, like other essential elements, is not set off by commas.

Use a comma to mark the end of a long introductory phrase or clause.

In this case the comma tells the reader: Now the real sentence is about to begin.

> Sailing into the Shoals and dropping anchor off Smuttynose, I felt like Columbus.

Use a comma to mark the end of a short introductory phrase or clause if you want want to approximate a conversational pause, or if you want to emphasize the introductory material so it won't be lost in the flow of the sentence.

> Anyway, Lew Hubbard told her she'd have to control the dog or lose it.
>
> For eleven years, Laura has dusted and sorted and polished these tables and chairs until they own her.

Either of these sentences could be written without the comma, depending on the rhythm you want to create, the words you wish to emphasize.

Use commas to indicate that someone is being addressed.

> *Not*: "Just what do you think you're up to Tom?"
> *But*: "Just what do you think you're up to, Tom?"

Use a comma before *and, but, or, for, yet, nor* if any of these words are used to connect independent clauses—that is, if the material before and the material after the connective each contain a subject and a verb.

> The moss has covered the ground completely, but I know the old house dump when I feel it.
>
> She brought him hot pastrami sandwiches from the delicatessen across the street, and he taught her to use Kodalith film and open the lens two extra f-stops to make the row of birch trees look etched against Lake Dwayne.

Use commas to separate adjectives in a series before a noun, unless the adjectives seem so closely related that you want them to work as one. (If you can replace the comma with "and" and the sentence makes sense, you've used the comma correctly.)

She stands at the kitchen door watching Dee—talented, articulate, charming Dee—at the end of a new Electrolux vacuum.

Notice that this sentence would make sense if the description of Dee read "talented and articulate and charming Dee"—
so the "and" substitution rule holds up.

In the following sentence, no commas are needed between
"two" and "white" or "white" and "quartz" because the three
words are working together to create one impression.

Two white quartz stones, veined, nearly as big as soccer balls,
balance on steps to nowhere because the house and barn
burned.

Again the "and" substitution rule holds: "two and white and
quartz stones" doesn't make sense.

This is tricky, because to place the comma or not place it
makes a substantial difference in the rhythm and meaning of
your sentence. Also, it is not usually a good idea to pile
modifiers in front of the noun. If you see a pile-up and are
debating whether to include commas or not, consider, too,
whether you need all those modifiers in the first place.

They are typical Sharon friends—funny, chatty, joyful women.

This could be written as follows, with one modifier before the
noun and two after to avoid a pile-up.

Sharon's friends tend to be funny women, chatty and joyful.

Hyphen   -

When modifiers do pile up before a noun, it is important that
the reader understand how they connect to one another and
to the noun. Hyphens, in these cases, let the reader know that
two or more words are functioning as one modifier and the
noun is still to come.

Pointy-headed dogs are not famous for brains.

When the same modifiers follow the noun, however, they
are not hyphenated.

The dog was pointy headed and not terribly intelligent.

Here's an example from John Updike's story "A & P":

... and then they all three of them went up to the cat-and-dog-food-breakfast-cereal-macaroni-rice-raisins-seasonings-spreads-spaghetti-soft-drinks-crackers-and-cookies aisle.

Sometimes the second half of the hyphenated modifier comes later, in which case you must dazzle your reader with the suspended hyphen.

I could not decide whether to ask for a three-, five-, or seven-day vacation.

Don't hyphenate superlatives (best, most), comparatives (more, less), or "ly" words even when they appear before a noun.

best loved quilt
more suitable attitude
carefully crafted box

Parentheses ( )

Like dashes, parentheses bring a degree of informality to the page. Use them sparingly. Too many make you appear scatter-brained or coy. Parentheses mean: I can't figure out where to put this exactly, it doesn't quite fit, so I'll slip it between these parentheses and hope you, dear reader, will absorb the information with the rest of the sentence.

Parentheses are great for varying the rhythm of sentences, subordinating information (this is important but not important enough to put in the base sentence), and creating a tone (an aside voice, a whispering confidante).

This was a woman whose grandchildren could set the barn afire without offending her (they didn't *mean* to), a woman who liked pastries for breakfast, a brandy or two before bed.

Sometimes, as in the example above, the parenthetical material is embedded in the sentence. In this case, even if the material is a complete sentence, do not capitalize and do not use end punctuation.

Not: ... without offending her (They didn't mean to.), a woman ...
Not: ... without offending her (they didn't mean to.), a woman. ...

Not: ... without offending her (They didn't mean to), a woman. ...

However, if the parenthetical material stands alone, as a separate sentence, capitalize and punctuate as you would any sentence.

This was a woman whose grandchildren could set the barn afire without offending her. ("They didn't mean to," she'd say.)

Exercises

1. Here's the lead to Susan Wheeler's story "Back Passage" with all the punctuation deleted. Add commas, periods, hyphens, dashes, whatever. Wheeler divided this into more than one paragraph. Where would you put the paragraph break or breaks? Play around with the possibilities. To see how the lead appeared when the story was published, turn to page 244.

I stand in the stern of the runabout wishing my husband would come to me he is up forward with Dave Fuller and with Nan his wife who is steering she's a brand new wife and eager my dufflebag rests on the floor by my feet I am abandoning my husband's three week vacation in Maine on our sailing cruiser and it feels like sin it demands explanation apology although technically I am only leaving a boat my husband feels betrayed because for years I've pretended I liked sailing for twenty three years I have lied and often believed the lie I have learned to steer a compass course make sandwiches on the wobbly cabin table while the boat heels I even took Power Squadron courses in a reformed barn that smelled like hay on damp days so I could navigate but finally last winter I admitted to myself and my husband that one week on the boat was enough that is why he doesn't stand beside me now though he glances at me from time to time but nervously as if checking to see I'm still here

2. Find a grammatically complex, emotionally powerful passage in one of your favorite stories. Type it. As you type, pay particular attention to the punctuation and think about the choices the writer made.

3. Choose a passage from one of your own stories. Retype it leaving out all the punctuation. Then punctuate it again with-

out looking at the original. Try to find different ways to join and separate the words.

Punctuation is all about choices and meaning. Playing with possibilities increases your knowledge and flexibility. As you read, become conscious of the choices other writers make, the rules they break, their favorite constructions, the patterns of their language.

Published Version of Lead to Wheeler's "Back Passage"

I stand in the stern of the runabout, wishing my husband would come to me. He is up forward with Dave Fuller and with Nan, his wife, who is steering. She's a brand new wife, and eager. My dufflebag rests on the floor by my feet. I am abandoning my husband's three-week vacation in Maine on our sailing cruiser, and it feels like sin. It demands explanation, apology, although technically I am only leaving a boat.

My husband feels betrayed because for years I've pretended I like sailing. For twenty-three years I have lied. And often believed the lie. I have learned to steer a compass course, make sandwiches on the wobbly cabin table while the boat heels—I even took Power Squadron courses in a reformed barn that smelled like hay on damp days so I could navigate—but finally, last winter, I admitted to myself and my husband that one week on the boat was enough. That is why he doesn't stand beside me now, though he glances at me from time to time—but nervously, as if checking to see if I'm still here.

Publishing

TRUST YOUR INSTINCTS. IF YOU HAVE DONE ALL YOU CAN WITH a story; if you have revised and polished, have read the final draft with objectivity and found the story stands up to tough scrutiny; if you're proud of your story, proud to put your name on it; if you want others to read the story and understand what you've come to understand through writing it—then it is time for publication in one form or another.

The final stage in the process of writing a story is showing it: first, perhaps, to your teacher, a member of your writing group, someone who is helping you write the story, and later to someone who's reading the story for its own sake, for herself, because she likes to read stories and here is one that interests her. Maybe afterward she'll tell you what she thinks of it. But typically she will not. Not if she lives three thousand miles away and reads your story in *Harpers*; not if she's a senior and you're a junior and maybe she's seen you on campus but she doesn't connect the face with the name in the school literary magazine. Response from readers at this stage is not terribly important; what matters is that you let the story go, you give it up to your audience.

Readings

Some writers love to read aloud; this is a form of publication. You might participate in readings at libraries, schools, nursing homes, cafes. Some of these readings are open to any writer (informal, step-up-to-the-microphone-and-read); some are by invitation only (though often it's not that hard to get invited). Writers groups sometimes sponsor readings by members. For goodness sake, if you want to read, organize a reading yourself. It's not hard: you need a room to hold it in, you need to let people know it's happening, you need to get some writers together and read.

Readings get your work out to the public; the response of listeners is immediate and usually gratifying. There's applause. Hardworking writers from time to time deserve applause.

Submitting to magazines

First, know the publication to which you're submitting your work; read it, read the fiction, be sure that your fiction would fit this market. When you're starting out, it's reasonable to submit to magazines with small circulations and, perhaps, a special interest in your work. If you're in school, by all means submit to your school journal or literary review. If your school doesn't have one, start one.

If your local or regional arts association puts out a journal and they limit themselves to, say, writers who live in Colorado, which you do, then your chances of publication are much greater than if you submitted to a magazine open to all writers.

Little or literary magazines, which are often associated with universities, writers groups, or arts projects, usually have small circulations but high standards. Typically they pay with one or two contributor's copies and a few words of praise. Often these magazines are quite beautiful—printed on heavy paper, carefully edited, sometimes illustrated. They are show-cases for your work that stay on readers' bookshelves for years and years, rather than being tossed in the trash or recycled like most commercial magazines.

Space for stories in commercial magazines is limited. Competition for that space and for the money these magazines pay writers is fierce. A commercial publication like The New Yorker or Redbook will receive thousands of unsolicited manuscripts each month. For new writers, the chance to publish in these high-circulation magazines is slim. Which doesn't mean you shouldn't submit. If you've read many issues and you think your story might fit, give it a try.

Send your story to one magazine at a time unless the magazine says it will consider a "multiple submission"; that is, a story that's been sent to several magazines at once.

Writer's Market and the more specialized *Novel and Short Story Writer's Market* are available at most libraries and bookstores. Published annually, they are full of information about both commercial and literary magazines. They tell you what kind of fiction the magazines are looking for, to whom you should mail your stories, how much the magazines pay, and much more. They also include detailed information on book publishers, contests and awards, and agents.

Poets and Writers magazine includes current market information, particularly on literary magazines, as well as good articles about writing.

Self-publishing

Some writers publish their work themselves, as a family project, group project, or business venture. One retirement association we know of sponsored a writing class for members, which led to a self-sustaining writing group, which led to a small magazine that they've been publishing now for several years.

If you're thinking big and you have the money, there are printers and subsidy publishers who will publish your work in book form. In this case you pay for publication up front and must do your own promotion and sales. *How to Get Happily Published* by Judith Applebaum and Nancy Evans is a good source of information on this subject. Be careful though— some writing contests, guarantees of publication, and so-called talent searches are just money-making schemes. In general, your writing is a valuable product. You should not have to pay anybody to print it. They should pay you.

Manuscript preparation

Don't try to impress editors with fancy paper or print. Let your story make an impression with plain, dark type on white paper, with margins about an inch all around, numbered pages, your name and address and telephone number on the first page at the top. Include a simple cover letter with the name of your story and a line or two saying where your work has been published (if it has been published). Don't try to sell your story; it will sell itself. Or not.

If you decide on multiple submissions, you must include that fact in your cover letter.

Send your story in a 9″ × 12″ envelope, unless it's under five pages, and then you can get away with a business-size envelope. Enclose a self-addressed, stamped envelope for return of your manuscript if it should be rejected.

Correspondence

Acceptance letters need no explanation. Read them, then go out and celebrate. Rejection letters might be a reason to celebrate too.

Form rejections mean virtually nothing. Throw them away.

Be encouraged, though, by a form rejection with a hand-written note at the bottom. An editor would not take the time to write a personal note unless something about your work appealed. A note that says, "Sorry, try us again," means just that.

Some writers are fortunate enough to receive personal rejection letters that critique the story. An editor may suggest you revise and resubmit or may recommend other markets.

Publication is in some ways a hit or miss operation—hitting the right editor at the right time with the right story. If you believe in a story, keep sending it out. It is not unusual for a writer to send a story to ten or twenty or more magazines before publication. Do not take rejection as a comment on the quality of your story; rejection often means this story does not fit this editor's idea of what belongs in this magazine at this time.

And that's probably all it means.

Don't agonize over each rejection. Do, however, send your story out to a new publication, that same day if possible.

It's a good idea to have several stories in circulation at a time so you don't concentrate all your hopes on one story.

If after you've had about fifteen stories rejected fifteen times each, then perhaps it is time for you to climb a mountain by yourself. Ask yourself: Do I want to continue to write fiction? Is my work good? Do I still believe in what I'm doing? This is a long, lonely, soul-searching climb. If your answers are yes, don't give up. Consider enrolling in a college writing course or a summer writer's workshop. Consider forming or joining a writer's group.

And keep writing.

LAST WORDS

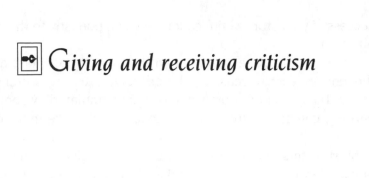

Giving and receiving criticism

WAIT UNTIL YOU'VE FINISHED A DRAFT OR SEVERAL DRAFTS OF A story before you show it to anyone. The dangers of showing a draft too soon include losing momentum because you've talked about your story instead of writing it, or getting criticism that deflates your enthusiasm. Some writers like to push a story as far as they can before they ask for help. Others would rather a share a story even though they know it has problems.

Find at least one critic who knows a lot about stories, is wise, compassionate, tough, honest, and constructive. This is probably not your mother, your spouse, or your best friend. You need someone who can be objective. Other writers usually make the best critics. If possible, find a fiction writer, join a writers group, or take a class.

Some writers like to show a story without commenting on its problems. They don't want to prejudice their readers. Other writers say you should tell your readers what worries you about your story and what you need to know about it. Rather than asking a general question like, "What do you think of this?" you can focus readers on trouble spots: "Do you think Bill's character is developed enough? What else do you want to know about him?" or, "Do you think the ending is too subtle? Do you know what's really going on in that scene? What do you think is really going on?"

Two of the best questions to ask are "Is this a story?" and "What do you think I'm trying to say here?" These get to the heart of storytelling; you can learn a lot about the success of your story when readers respond honestly to these questions.

Some people write best in a writing workshop where, at the end of each discussion, blood runs over the writer's shoes. The gladiator approach. If you are stimulated by competitive, combative criticism, get together with like-minded people.

Most writers, though, need nurturing and thrive on earned praise. They're unsure, jittery, and learn from encouragement.

The object of workshops or exchanges is to help writers improve their work. The worst response a writer can get is silence. The second worst is "I like it," or "I don't like it," with no elaboration. When you criticize, learn to preface your criticism with "It seems to me . . ." or "I think . . ." acknowledging the possibility of other responses. If someone says to you, "This is terrific," or "This stinks," know this is only one opinion.

Avoid playing God or hanging around critics who play God. Professional critics often disagree about a writer's work. You and your friends will disagree. Eventually each writer must decide what criticism makes sense and is useful, and what doesn't. Each writer must decide what criticism to accept and what to dismiss.

Don't give in to modesty. Of course people new to fiction fear saying something stupid or foolish or wrong. We all say stupid, foolish, wrong things about stories. As you practice critiquing, you'll become better at it—though you'll still make mistakes. So will your friends. And if you're in a class, so will your teacher. Remember the writer won't be ruined by one misguided remark from you. You're learning and so is the writer. Ask yourself how you would feel if, when your story is discussed, no one dares say anything for fear of being wrong. Be generous with your criticism. Eventually these skills will pay off: as you become a better critic of other writers' stories, you'll learn to become your own best critic.

Assume that everyone who is swapping drafts of stories is trying to improve. Before you offer criticism, think: is this going to help? And if you think it will help, speak up, knowing that everyone, unless he's insufferable, is anxious about his ability and his work.

First point out what works in a story. This is not a goody-goody activity. It's essential. Most new writers don't recognize what's best in their writing. They need to know so they can count on their strengths and use them again and again. They need to know where they can be confident.

Once strengths are pointed out, the writer will often on her own recognize what doesn't work. If not, readers can point out flaws. For each flaw, brainstorm solutions. Again, take your role of critic seriously: the solution to your friend's problem in this story may become the solution to a problem of your own later on.

Don't say: "I like the lead *but*. . . ." Say, "I like the lead." Then pause. Let the praise sink in. Then say why you like it. Say what else you like in the story. Later you can and should say, "I had trouble with this," or "This may be my problem, but I was confused here."

If you think a story is terrible, you can always find a detail, a sentence, a phrase that worked. Mention it. Then you do have the obligation to say something like, "I'm sorry, but for me this story isn't working." And say why. If you've seen another story you liked by the same writer, tell him that you liked that story much better than this one. Phrase the criticism so that the writer knows you're on his side. That you're trying to help, you're rooting for him. Always criticize the story, not the person who wrote it. Not: "You really messed up the lead," but: "I found the lead slow. How about starting on page three, paragraph four?"

The story may seem a disaster to you—sentimental or silly or melodramatic. It's hard to say these things, but you'll have to if you want to help the writer. Instead of saying, "This is sentimental slop," or, "This is a bore," you can say: "This is a love story and love stories can easily fall into sentiment. I feel yours does. I think you need to watch for this." Then point out several places that are sentimental. You don't have to read each embarrassing word or phrase. One or two will be enough. Then tell the writer to check for sentiment all

255

through. Then keep quiet a minute or two to see what the writer has to say.

Don't over praise. Yes, be enthusiastic, tell the writer you love or like this or that, but be sure to point out areas that need work.

After you've received advice about your story, take a long walk. You'll find that the comments by people who seemed to get at the heart of your story will be most helpful and will stay with you. Let irrelevant remarks, or remarks that seem wrong somehow, slip away. And as you think about the good and not-so-good parts of your story, ask yourself: What do I want *now* for my story? What most interests me *now*? What interests you most now may not be what interested you most when you began your story. You'll rethink with that "now" in mind.

Pay attention to how you feel after a story of yours has been critiqued by an individual or by a group in a workshop. Do you feel like writing? Do you want to go back and revise or start a new story? Is there a sense of people supporting each other? Do you have a better idea of your strengths and weaknesses, a sense of direction? Or do you feel like leaping from the bridge?

If you're in a workshop or group where people slash and stab, or if they only praise, and if this depresses you, for heaven's sake leave the workshop. Don't set yourself back months in your writing progress. If, however, you've been hurt by some severe criticism, but you feel after thinking about it that your story really was trite or melodramatic, or that you do use clichés or stereotyped characters, then put away the stories that don't work. Curse. Cry. Curse again. And start another story.

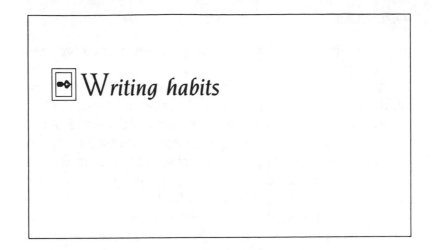

Writing habits

WRITERS WRITE. IT'S A JOB, AND HARD WORK. FOR SOME REASON, a lot of people believe writers receive these mystical inspirations and sit down only when they feel like it and record voices. Yes, there is inspiration, but it tends to come to writers who have worked for long hours and laid the groundwork for it. Writing takes discipline. You write one word after another word, one hour after another hour, day after day.

Fiction writers often write several hours a day most days every week. The minimum seems to be three or four hours a day. Some people write eight hours a day. Most writers also teach or work at other jobs to earn a steady income. If they teach in colleges, they often write mornings and teach several afternoons a week. People with jobs outside colleges carry drafts around in their heads and will sometimes write evenings or get up at four or five in the morning to put in their time. Some cram their work into four days a week and write the other three. Still others reserve weekends for writing.

Why should fiction writing take so much time? Partly it's because we're inventing our worlds as well as describing them; partly it's because we're working to see as deeply as we can into our main characters' minds or souls or psyches; and like all writers, we work to make the words right. Just as a person in therapy isn't magically given insight after one visit, writers need a great deal of time—in this case writing and rewriting time—to learn about their characters. Writers need to think, mull, speculate, despair, get excited, wonder, and revise.

Most writers work up to sustained writing times. You might start by committing yourself to an hour or an hour and a half a day for five days a week for one month. At the end of the month, decide if you want to keep going another month at this pace, or quit writing and be normal. At month three, you might write for two hours a day for perhaps six days a week and promise yourself you'll do this for four more weeks, and so forth. Perhaps you have a full-time job and are exhausted when you come home. You might decide that some people play golf on weekends, but you'll write. You could write from eight to noon on Saturdays and Sundays. Be realistic about the amount of time you can spend at first. Don't set up a schedule that's bound to fail. If half an hour a day, three days a week feels right as a starter, fine. If it's a quota—a page a day for a week or a month—fine. But stick to it.

This is why writers establish schedules. When they know they'll face the word processor or a blank page and a pencil at seven a.m. each morning for a month, their minds become used to focusing on their stories at that hour and they waste less time than if they were to write at different times. A schedule is also important because it's easy to let an hour slip away here, a day there.

When you write, don't leave your room except to go to the bathroom. If you can't work on a story, you can always brainstorm ideas in a journal, or write about a character whom you can't stand, or describe a troublesome event in your life and start playing "what if" with it. You can try some of the exercises in this book. Stories often emerge from journal entries.

When you set this time aside for writing, don't answer the telephone or the door. Don't get up to do the laundry or put new spark plugs in your car. Sit at your desk. Write when you're sick, in love, or in grief. Write when you're going to take a trip across the country the next day or when you're going to have your boss over for supper that night. A fever of over a hundred and one degrees is grounds for not writing. But you should work on the day of a wedding or funeral unless you're a major participant. Plan dentist and doctor appointments for times when you aren't writing.

Don't let friends or family interfere. It's extraordinary how roommates, spouses, and parents can resent and infringe on your writing time. "Can't you just this *once* give up a morning and go downtown with me?" No. You can't. They won't like you for saying no, especially at first. They may not understand why it takes so long to get published. Perhaps they would tolerate your habit if you were a house painter who could show them a freshly painted room instead of saying, "I don't like to talk about what I'm writing," a reply which non-writers feel is precious and irritating. But most of us *can't* talk about our writing. We need to tell people we must save our thoughts about our stories for our pages and be tough enough not to let anyone stop us.

Some new writers have the support of people who live with them. If you don't, explain politely once or twice that you have to be selfish. Show people this guide if you think it will help. Show them some of the entries in *Writers at Work: The Paris Interviews*.

It takes years to learn the craft. There is even a book of interviews with writers, edited by George Garrett, called *Craft So Hard To Learn*.

Many people have talent and brains. What separates those who publish and those who don't is, often, discipline. But a wonderful thing happens to many writers after they get hooked on writing. It's harder to miss a day of writing than it is to write.

⊷ Exercise

Buy a journal to keep your work moving. This will be for warm-up writing, exercises, quotes, newspaper cutouts, and comments on your writing. This will be your idea book. Write in it often, a little, or a lot. When you hit rough going with a story, you'll do more journal work; it will help you find your way.

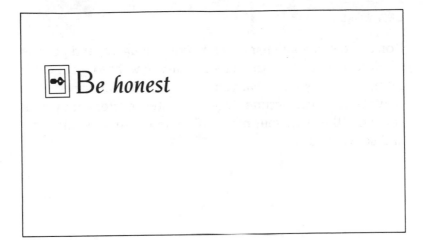

Be honest

GOOD WRITERS HAVE INTEGRITY AND IT SHOWS. IT SHOWS IN the language, which is exact and original and often delights us. It shows in the main characters, who are round and complex. It shows in the insights, which are surprising and important. It shows in every line.

Be accurate. Be the kind of writer whom readers trust. Check facts. Use libraries, call policemen, doctors, gardeners—whomever you need—to get your information correct.

Use words honestly. Be exact. Don't say. "Her mother screamed at her," when the reader suspects the mother just raised her voice. Avoid clichés and glib expressions. Readers want to trust a writer's vision, to feel the clarity and originality of that vision. This includes details. We've all read stories where writers seem content to grab the first details they think of: for instance, "Her palms were sweating as she gripped the wheel and her knuckles turned white." That's overused, stale. Look for fresh details that reveal characters and places as distinctive, that reveal theme, that are memorable, and that draw the reader in.

Be honest as you explore your main characters. Like real people, they aren't all good or all bad. Pay attention to their complexities. And never force them into behaviors merely to satisfy your preconceived notion of plot. Let them be rich, complex. Let them surprise you.

Often we identify with our main characters, so when they misbehave or disappoint us, we may feel threatened, exposed.

Don't sweeten your character's words, thoughts, and actions to protect yourself, or to protect what you want for your character, or to play into what you think your reader wants.

Write one clear, accurate, honest sentence after another. As you write this way, your prose will gain depth and authority, and so will you.

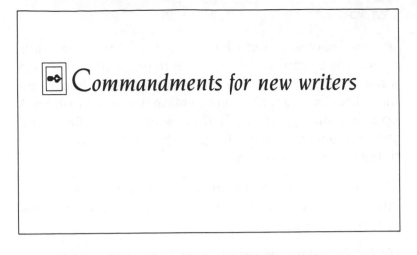 Commandments for new writers

WE'VE GIVEN MOST OF THIS ADVICE ELSEWHERE IN THIS BOOK. But these points are so important we wanted to put them altogether as a reminder.

1. Write every day. If possible, write at the same time every day.

2. As you write, focus on learning about your main character; work for insights into your character.

3. If you're interested in style, buy a hat. If you focus on your story, on your character who is in trouble, on discovering the truth, style will emerge. If you worry about style as you write, your story will stink of self-consciousness.

4. Make sure readers know where they are in time and place.

5. Be clear. Don't be elliptical, vague or fuzzy. Be clear.

6. Be direct, straightforward, and honest. Don't be coy, cute, sentimental, melodramatic, or smart alecky.

7. Don't withold important information in order to lure your reader on. Yes, readers want to find out what happens next, but the suspense should involve important matters, not such things as whether the main character is a man or a parrot.

8. Give readers credit—for wanting to know the truth, for wanting to know how a character thinks, feels, and acts in a specific, clearly rendered conflict. Don't rely on cheesy gimmicks like flood, famine, or fire to make the reader read on. A note here though: There's nothing wrong with a flood or a stabbing. But your emphasis should be on the *meaning* of the trouble, its reverberations.

9. Make sure something happens in a story. This may be internal, external, or both, but make sure somebody or something somehow changes.

10. Catch readers and get a fast start on your story by plunging into the middle of conflict, conversation, action, thought, drama.

11. If you're wondering which details to include, use theme as the litmus test: what is this story really about? Uncertainty about details may also be a sign that you've lost sight of the specific conflict. If someone holds a gun to your main character's head, who cares about the color of the assailant's shoelaces? What counts is that finger on the trigger.

12. Know what your story means. You likely won't know in the first draft, but eventually you must. Make everything in the story work for that theme.

13. Beware of starting a story to prove something (this is how a woman reacts to an abusive husband) or to illustrate a concept (racial prejudice is ugly). Start with characters in conflict—specific conflict. Write to see what happens.

14. Don't use scenes, or dialogue within scenes, to deliver background information that could be more efficiently delivered straight out.

15. In final drafts, consider yourself a guide. Your readers know nothing of your territory. Take them by the hand and lead them. Readers aren't idiots, but they are new to your world.

16. If your writing feels feeble, if you feel confidence slipping away, stop. Let the critic in your head write a letter articulating all that you think is wrong with your work. Then, when you see how ridiculous those assertions are, write back as though you were your own best friend. Have confidence.

17. Keep writing.

Suggested Readings

MANY OF THE STORIES WE REFER TO IN THIS BOOK ARE included in *The Story and Its Writer*, edited by Ann Charters (Bedford Books, 1991). *The Best American Short Stories* series (Houghton Mifflin) and the O. *Henry Awards* series come out each year, are published in paperback, and include outstanding stories from both commercial and literary magazines. The *Pushcart Prize* series (Penguin) features poetry and fiction from small presses. There are several collections of stories by women including *Women and Fiction* (Mentor), edited by Susan Cahill and *Sisters of the Earth*, edited by Lorraine Anderson. Don't miss the *Graywolf Annuals*, including *Graywolf Annual 2: Short Stories by Women*, *Graywolf Annual 4: Short Stories by Men*, and *Graywolf Annual 6: Stories from the Rest of the World*.

Read fiction in literary quarterlies such as *The North American Review*, *The Paris Review*, *The Black Warrior Review*, *Ploughshares*, *Willow Springs*, *The Southern Review*, *The Northwest Review*, *The New England Review*, *Potato Eyes*, *Story Quarterly*, *Story*, *Grand Street*. There are hundreds of fine literary magazines where you'll find wonderful fiction and where you may likely want someday to send your stories for publication. You can find these in many university or college libraries and in some bookstores. In the back of *The Best American Short Stories*, put out in paperback by Houghton Mifflin Company each year, you'll find names and addresses of many quarterlies. These are the magazines where you'll find some of the best fiction written today. Subscribe to one or two of them. Read stories in commercial magazines such as *The Atlantic Monthly*, *Harpers*, *The New Yorker*, *Redbook*, *Esquire*.

When you find a writer whose work you admire in an anthology or magazine, you'll want to read more. Collections are available for most of the writers we discuss.

It's risky recommending books. Because of space we must leave out wonderful writers, and most writers hate to be categorized. And yet, we suggest stories and writers to our students. We need to point out to you, though, that the authors we recommend cannot be confined to the narrow boxes in which we're forced to place them here because of space constraints.

If you need to write about characters who have backgrounds, histories, and experiences that are complex and may cause them to dwell on the past, trying to make sense of things, then these writers and or stories may help you: Ethan Canin's "Emperor of the Air," from his collection *Emperor of the Air*; many of Andre Dubus' stories in *Adultery and Other Choices* and *Finding a Girl in America* (his main characters often reflect in long extended passages); William Faulkner's "Wash" in his collected stories; Toni Morrison's novel, *Song of Solomon*; Alice Munro's "Friend of My Youth" from the collection by that same name; Gloria Naylor's *Mama Day* or *Women of Brewster Place*; Flannery O'Connor's "Everything That Rises Must Converge" in her collection of stories.

If you want to write about a character who feels things intensely, receives impressions all in a rush with moments of revelation that seem more like sudden intuitions or gifts than conclusions arrived at slowly, logically, you may be helped by reading Virginia Woolf's story, "The New Dress" in her collection, *A Haunted House and Other Stories*. Mark Helprin's "Schreuderspitze" in his *Ellis Island and Other Stories* contains a dream at the end that heals a main character. This is dangerous: we're warned about dreams being too symbolic and obvious, and the warning is valid. However, in this story, the dream works. Read Helprin's "White Gardens" in this collection, too; it's an almost mystical story, as is Sherwood Anderson's "Death in the Woods." Read Alice Walker's "Roselily."

If you have a story that wants to be told in a linear way, that moves forward in a straight narrative line to the end, read "The Ledge," by Lawrence Sargeant Hall. (See our guide "Finding Meaning" for a more in-depth discussion of this story.) Read Hemingway's Nick Adams stories, in *The Short Stories of Ernest Hemingway*, and Tobias Wolff's "Hunters in the Snow."

We discussed circular, looping stories in our guide "Time Frames and Story Shapes." If you have a story you want to write in which the past and future seem cradled in time present, read Gabriel García Márquez' novella, *Chronicle of a Death Foretold*. He'll go forward and back twenty-five years in one sentence and never confuse readers. He's extraordinarily agile. Throughout Alice McDermott's short novel, *That Night*, the first-person narrator keeps remembering and referring to a fight that's described in the first few pages. Peter Taylor's story, "The Gift of the Prodigal" takes place in only a few minutes with extraordinary loops into the past. It's a story where the beginning and the end are almost simultaneous. Read Virginia Woolf's "The New Dress."

If you want to rely heavily on a surface rendering of events, trusting that if you do this well enough, there will be deeper reverberations, read Joan Didion's very short novel, *Play It As It Lays*. Read Tim O'Brien, Raymond Carver, Ann Beattie, Bobbie Ann Mason, and Ernest Hemingway's Nick Adams stories. These writers do go into their characters' thoughts and backgrounds, but on the whole, they tend to devote less space to them than do such writers as Margaret Atwood, Willa Cather, John Cheever, Anton Chekhov, Margaret Laurence, Alice Munro, Jane Smiley, John Updike, and Theodore Weesner.

If you want to study a writer who comments on what's happening in her stories, often saying things her characters would not or could not say, read Flannery O'Connor's short stories, including "A Good Man Is Hard To Find" and "Everything That Rises Must Converge." In the novel, *At Weddings and Wakes*, Alice McDermott comments with great wisdom on the lives of her characters as does Isak Dinesen in "Sorrow Acre," from her collection *A Winter's Tale*.

First-person stories allow the narrators to comment exten-sively if they wish: for examples of this see "Friend of My Youth," a story in Alice Munro's collection, *Friend of My Youth*, or, again, Alice McDermott's *That Night*, and Mark Helprin's short story "Tamar," in *Ellis Island and Other Stories*. Stories where first-person adult narrators recall the past allow writers to explore how the character felt at the time the events took place as well as now, as the characters reflect back on what happened. (See our guide "Choosing the Past or Present Tense")

For stories that contain violence, read William Faulkner's and Flannery O'Connor's short story collections. Read Toni Morrison's novel, *The Bluest Eye*, and Tim O'Brien's *The Things They Carried*. Read Andre Dubus' short story, "The Curse," and Judith Rossner's novel, *Looking for Mr. Goodbar*.

For a collection of short stories about characters who are gay or lesbian, read *The Faber Book of Gay Short Fiction*, edited by Edmund White and published by Faber & Faber, and Madelyn Arudd's *On Ships at Sea*.

Gabriel García Márquez often mingles realistic and fantas-tic details in his novel *Chronicle of a Death Foretold* and in his short stories. Carlos Fuentes's later stories, like Márquez's, are concerned with the extraordinary in everyday experiences. Isabel Allende's novel, *Eva Luna*, is filled with the extraordi-nary. In *Floating in My Mother's Palm*, many of Ursula Hegi's stories could be labeled—though we dislike labels—magical realism. A quick warning is called for here. Magical realism is not something pasted on to a story for effect. Rather, it results from a writer's or her characters' ways of seeing the world, a belief that dreams, fantasies, superstitions, and sudden intu-itions and revelations are as real as what most of us call "the real world," and that they need to be included in fiction.

There are a number of literary science fiction writers such as Ursula LeGuin and Angela Carter, but we must caution you again here. For your first stories we suggest you stay close to your world, to what you know, to your experiences, and to your ways of seeing. It's hard to learn writing skills, and harder still when you have to first, invent a world, and then describe it vividly.

Here are some names of other writers you may want to read. These are only a few of the writers we enjoy, but there are enough here to get you started. Most of them have collections of short stories and novels; some have published only novels or story collections. Of course, there are the classic works of Sherwood Anderson, Willa Cather, Anton Chekhov, Kate Chopin, Colette, Joseph Conrad, Stephen Crane, Isak Dinesen, William Faulkner, F. Scott Fitzgerald, Gustave Flaubert, Mary E. Wilkins Freeman, Charlotte Perkins Gilman, Nikolai Gogol, Ernest Hemingway, Zora Neale Hurston, Franz Kafka, Henry James, Sarah Orne Jewett, James Joyce, Franz Kafka, Katherine Mansfield, Flannery O'Connor, Katherine Anne Porter, Edith Wharton, Virginia Woolf.

Also available in most libraries and bookstores are collections from well-known writers who are more recently published, such as Alice Adams, James Baldwin, Toni Cade Bambara, Saul Bellow, Jorge Luis Borges, Gwendolyn Brooks, Rita Mae Brown, Rosellen Brown, Italo Calvino, Albert Camus, Truman Capote, Joan Chase, Margaret-Love Denman, Margaret Drabble, Ralph Ellison, Louise Erdrich, Mavis Gallant, John Gardner, Mark Helprin, George Garrett, Kaye Gibbons, Ellen Gilchrist, Nadine Gordimer, Amy Hempel, Yussef Idriss, Jamaica Kincaid, Milan Kundera, David Leavitt, Ursula LeGuin, Doris Lessing, Bernard Malamud, William Maxwell, Carson McCullers, Leonard Michaels, Susan Minot, Yukio Mishima, Bharati Mukherjee, Vladimir Nabakov, Joyce Carol Oates, Edna O'Brien, Tillie Olsen, Cynthia Ozick, Pamela Painter, Grace Paley, Gail Pass, Mary Robison, Leslie Marmon Silko, Isaac Bashevis Singer, Mark Smith, Susan Sontag, John Steinbeck, Edmund White, Hwang Sun-Won, Amy Tan, William Trevor, Amos Tutucla, Luisa Valenzuela, Robert Penn Warren, Fay Weldon, Eudora Welty, Barbara Wright, Nathanael West, John Edgar Wideman, Elie Wiesel, Joy Williams, Thomas Williams, Robley Wilson, Tobias Wolff, Hilma Wolitzer, Richard Wright, John Yount, Marguerite Yourcenar.

You will discover many writers we haven't had room to discuss here. Read book reviews. The Sunday *New York Times*

Book Review discusses many books each week. Read stories in commercial and literary magazines. Ask your librarian or an English teacher to recommend books. Tell that person what you're looking for, and what writers you've liked so far. You might want to ask a librarian to recommend, say, a regional writer, a lesbian writer, a Canadian or South African writer, a writer whose characters may have specific religious or philosophical beliefs similar to your own. You'll be helped by reading writers who have solved some of the problems you face and who write about material somewhat like your own, but of course you'll also need to study writers who write about people and situations very different from yours.

REFERENCES

Agee, James. 1968. A *death in the family*, 224–5. New York: Avon.

Allen, Woody. 1991. The Kugelmass episode. In *The story and its writer*, edited by Ann Charters, 20. Boston: Bedford Books of St. Martin's Press.

Allende, Isabel. 1989. *Eva Luna*. New York: Bantam.

Anderson, Sherwood. 1988. *Winesburg, Ohio*. New York: Penguin.

————. 1991. Death in the woods. In *The story and its writer*, edited by Ann Charters. Boston: Bedford Books of St. Martin's Press.

Applebaum, Judith and Nancy Evans. 1982. *How to get happily published*. New York: New American Library.

Arnold, Madelyn. 1991. On ships at sea, New York: St. Martin's Press.

Bambara, Toni Cade. 1991. The hammer man. In *The story and its writer*, edited by Ann Charters, 82. Boston: Bedford Books of St. Martin's Press.

————. 1972. The lesson. In *Gorilla, my love*, 85. New York: Vintage/ Random House.

Baxter, Charles. 1986. The cliff. In *Sudden fiction*, edited by Robert Shepard and James Thomas. Salt Lake City: Peregrine Smith.

Beattie, Ann. 1986. Janus. In *The best short stories of* 1986, edited by Raymond Carver. Boston: Houghton Mifflin.

REFERENCES

Bellow, Saul. 1978 Leaving the yellow house. In *The Norton anthology of short fiction*, 3rd edition, edited by R.V. Cassill, 54–55. New York: W.W. Norton & Co.

Bernays, Anne and Pamela Painter. 1990. *What if*. New York: Harper Collins.

Calvino, Italo. 1977. *The baron in the trees*. New York: Harcourt Brace Jovanovich.

Camus, Albert. 1988. *The stranger*. New York: Knopf.

Canin, Ethan. 1988. Emperor of the air. In *Emperor of the air*, 8. Boston: Houghton Mifflin.

Capote, Truman. 1966. My side of the matter. In *Points of view*, edited by James Moffett and Kenneth R. McElheny. New York: Mentor from New American Library.

Carver, Raymond. *Shoptalk*, edited by Donald M. Murray, 181. Portsmouth, NH: Boynton/Cook.

————. 1988. What we talk about when we talk about love. In *Where I'm calling from*. New York: Vintage of Random House.

Cheever, John. 1978. The lowboy. In *The stories of John Cheever*. New York: Knopf.

————. 1978. Torch song. In *The stories of John Cheever*. New York: Knopf.

Chekhov, Anton. *Shoptalk*, 149, edited by Donald M. Murray. Portsmouth, NH: Boynton/Cook.

————. 1991. The lady with the pet dog. In *The story and its writer*, edited by Ann Charters, 258. Boston: Bedford Books of St. Martin's Press.

Chicago manual of style, 13th edition. 1982. Chicago: University of Chicago Press.

Chopin, Kate. 1991. The story of an hour. In *The story and its writer*, edited by Ann Charters. Boston: Bedford Books of St. Martin's Press.

Chute, Carolyn. 1985. *The beans of Egypt, Maine*, 3. New York: Ticknor and Fields.

Connors, Robert and Andrea Lunsford. 1989. *The St. Martin's handbook*. Boston: St. Martin's Press.

Costello, Mark. 1973. Murphy's Xmas. In *The Murphy stories*. Urbana: University of Illinois Press.

Denman, Margaret-Love. 1992. A *scrambling after circumstance*, 1. New York: Penguin Books.

Didion, Joan. 1978. *Play it as it lays*. 23. New York: Pocket Books.

Dinesen, Isak. 1961. Sorrow acre. *Winter's tales*. New York: Vintage of Random House.

Dubus, Andre. 1977. *Adultery and other choices*. Boston: Godine.

————. 1981. *Finding a girl in America*. Boston: Godine.

————. 1991. The curse. In *The story and its writer*, edited by Ann Charters. Boston: Bedford Books of St. Martin's Press.

Erdrich, Louise. 1984. *Love medicine*, 4–5. New York: Holt Rinehart Winston.

Faulkner, William. 1943. Barn burning. In *The collected stories of William Faulkner*, 5–6 New York: Random House.

————. 1943. The brooch. In *The collected stories of William Faulkner*. New York: Random House.

————. 1943. Dry September. In *The collected stories of William Faulkner*. New York: Random House.

————. 1943. Wash. In *The collected stories of William Faulkner*. New York: Random House.

————. 1988. A rose for Emily. In *The story*, edited by David Bergman. Boston: Houghton Mifflin.

Flaubert, Gustave. 1991. A simple heart. In *The story and its writer*, edited by Ann Charters, 468. Boston: Bedford Books of St. Martin's Press.

REFERENCES

García Márquez, Gabriel. 1982. *chronicle of a death foretold*. New York: Ballantine of Random House.

——. 1984. A very old man with enormous wings. In *Collected stories*. New York: Harper and Row.

Garrett, George. 1972. *Craft so hard to learn*. New York: Morrow Paperback Editions, William Morrow & Company.

——. 1971. *Death of the Fox*. New York: Doubleday and Company.

Gilchrist, Ellen. 1981. There's a garden of Eden. In *In the land of dreamy dreams*, 38. New York: Little Brown.

Goldberg, Natalie. 1986. *Writing down the bones*. Boston: Shambhala Publications.

Hall, Lawrence Sargeant. 1971. The ledge. In *Stories that count*. New York: Holt, Rinehart & Winston.

Hegi, Ursula. 1990. *Floating in my mother's palm*. New York: Poseidon Press.

——. 1990. Saving a life, 185. In *Floating in my mother's palm*. New York: Poseidon Press.

Helprin, Mark. 1982. *Ellis Island and other stories*. New York: Dell.

——. 1982. Tamar. *Ellis Island and other stories*. New York: Dell.

——. 1982. Schreuderspitz. In *Ellis Island and other stories*. New York: Dell.

——. 1982. White gardens. *Ellis Island and other stories*. New York: Dell.

Hemingway, Ernest. 1969. A *farewell to arms*. New York: Scribners.

——. 1970. Cat in the rain. In *In our time*. New York: Scribners.

——. 1987. *The short stories of Ernest Hemingway*. New York: Macmillan.

——. 1987. A clean, well-lighted place. In *The short stories of Ernest Hemingway*. New York: Macmillan.

————. 1991. Hills like white elephants. In *The story and its writer*, edited by Ann Charters. Boston: Bedford Books of St. Martin's Press.

Jackson, Shirley. 1991. The lottery. In *The story and its writer*, edited by Ann Charters. New York: Bedford Books of St. Martin's Press.

————. 1991. The morning of June 28, 1948 and The lottery. In *The story and its writer*, edited by Ann Charters. Boston: Bedford Books of St. Martin's press.

Joyce, James. 1954. The dead. In *The Dubliners*, 288. New York: Modern Library of Random House.

————. 1954. Eveline. In *The Dubliners*, 42. New York: Modern Library of Random House.

Kincaid, Jamaica. 1987. Girl. In *Writing Fiction* by Janet Burroway, 133. Boston: Little, Brown.

Lawrence, D.H. 1991. The rocking-horse winner. In *The story and its writer*, edited by Ann Charters, 813. Boston: Bedford Books of St. Martin's Press.

Leavitt, David. 1991. Territory. In *The story and its writer*, edited by Ann Charters, 825. Boston: Bedford Books of St. Martin's Press.

Mason, Bobbie Ann. 1982. Shiloh. In *Shiloh and other stories*, 1. New York: Perennial Library of Harper and Row.

McDermott, Alice. 1987. *That night*, 4 and 5. New York: Farrar, Straus & Giroux.

————. 1992. *At weddings and wakes*. New York: Farrar, Straus & Giroux.

McInerney, Jay. 1984. *Bright lights, big city*. New York: Vintage of Random House.

Minot, Susan. 1991. Lust. In *The story and its writer*, edited by Ann Charters, 988. Boston: Bedford Books of St. Martin's Press.

Morris, Rebecca. 1975. The good humor man. In *Bitches and sad ladies*, 251. New York: Dell.

REFERENCES

Morrison, Toni. 1972. *The bluest eye*. New York: Washington Square Press of Simon and Schuster.

————. 1977. *Song of Solomon*. New York: Random House.

Munro, Alice. 1990. Friend of my youth. In *Friend of my youth*. New York: Knopf.

————. 1991. The turkey season. In *Moons of Jupiter*, 63. New York: Vintage Books of Random House.

Murray, Donald. M. 1990. *Shoptalk: learning to write with writers*, 149. Portsmouth, NH: Boynton/Cook.

Naylor, Gloria. 1985. *The women of Brewster Place*. New York: Penguin.

————. 1989. *Mama day*. New York: Vintage of Random House.

Novel and short story writer's market. Annual. Cincinnati: Writer's Digest Books.

O'Brien, Tim. 1990. The things they carried. In *The things they carried*, 6. New York: Penguin.

O'Connor, Flannery. 1991. A good man is hard to find. In *The story and its writer*, edited by Ann Charters, 1097. Boston: Bedford Books of St. Martin's Press.

————. 1991. Everything that rises must converge. In *The story and its writer*, edited by Ann Charters, 1085–1097. Boston: Bedford Books of St. Martin's Press.

Olsen, Tillie. 1978. I stand here ironing. In *Tell me a riddle*. New York: Dell.

Ozick, Cynthia. 1991. The shawl. In *The story and its writer*, edited by Ann Charters. Boston: Bedford Books of St. Martin's Press.

Paley, Grace. 1987. The pale pink roast. In *The little disturbances of man*. New York: Penguin.

————. 1991. A conversation with my father. In *The story and its writer*, edited by Ann Charters. Boston: Bedford Books of St. Martin's Press.

Pierce, Anne Whitney. December, 1989. Sans homme. In *The North American review*, 25. Cedar Falls: University of Northern Iowa.

Porter, Katherine Anne. 1979. María Concepcíon. In *The collected stories of Katherine Anne Porter*, 3–21. New York: Harcourt Brace Jovanovich.

———. 1979. Rope. In *The collected stories of Katherine Anne Porter*, 42. New York: Harcourt Brace Jovanovich.

Robinson, Marilynne. 1987. *Housekeeping*. New York: Bantam.

Robinson, Mary. 1986. Yours. In *Sudden fiction*, edited by Robert Shepard and James Thomas. Salt Lake City, UT: Peregrine Smith.

Rule, Rebecca. 1992. Heritage. In *Wood heat*. Troy, ME: Nightshade Press.

———. 1992. The man who saw bigfoot. In *Wood heat*. Troy, ME: Nightshade Press.

———. 1992. Wood heat, no backup. In *The Nightshade short story reader*, 83. Troy, ME: Nightshade Press.

Selzer, Richard. 1987. The masked marvel's last toehold. In *Writing fiction* by Janet Burroway, 258, 260. Boston: Little Brown.

Shepard, Robert and James Thomas, editors. 1986. *Sudden fiction*. Salt Lake City UT: Peregrine Smith.

Silko, Leslie Marmon. 1991. Yellow woman. In *The story and its writer*, edited by Ann Charters, 1158. Boston: Bedford Books of St. Martin's Press.

Smiley, Jane. 1985. Lily. In *The best American short stories of 1985*, edited by Gail Godwin. Boston: Houghton Mifflin.

Strunk, William Jr. and E. B. White. 1979. *The elements of style*. New York: Macmillan.

Tan, Amy. 1989. *The joy luck club*, 133. New York: Ballantine of Random House.

Taylor, Peter. 1987. The gift of the prodigal. In *Writing fiction* by Janet Burroway, 291–305. Boston: Little, Brown.

Tsushima, Yoko. 1989. The silent traders. In *Stories from the rest of the world*, 1–11. St. Paul, MN: Graywolf.

REFERENCES

Updike, John. 1991. A & P. In *The story and its writer*, edited by Ann Charters, 1274. Boston: Bedford Books of St. Martin's Press.

Walker, Alice. 1981. Petunias. In *You can't keep a good woman down*, 40. New York: Harcourt Brace Jovanovich.

———. 1991. Roselily. In *The story and its writer*, edited by Ann Charters, 1296. Boston: Bedford Books of St. Martin's Press.

Warren, Robert Penn. 1989. *Robert Penn Warren: New and selected essays.* New York: Random House.

Wheeler, Susan. Summer, 1978. Hangin' on the wall. In *The North American Review*, 21, 26. Cedar Falls: University of Northern Iowa.

———. Spring, 1990 Back passage. In *The Lyndon Review*, 36. Lyndonville, VT: Lyndon State College.

White, Edmund, editor. 1991. *The Faber book of gay short fiction.* Colchester, VT: Faber and Faber.

Williams, Joy. 1990. Health. In *The best short stories of the eighties*, edited by Shannon Ravenel, 241. Boston: Houghton Mifflin.

Wolitzer, Hilma. 1975 The sex maniac. In *Bitches and sad ladies*, 62. New York: Dell.

Wolff, Tobias. 1991. Hunters in the snow. In *The story and its writer*, edited by Ann Charters. Boston: Bedford Books of St. Martin's Press.

Woolf, Virginia. 1972. The new dress. In *A haunted house and other stories*, 47. New York: A Harvest Book/Harcourt Brace Jovanovich.

Wright, Richard. 1988. The man who was almost a man. In *The story*, edited by David Bergman. New York: Macmillan.

Writers at work: The Paris Review interviews. Annual. Edited by George Plimpton. New York: Viking.

Writers' Market. Annual. Cincinnati: Writer's Digest Books.

Yount, John. 1973. *The trapper's last shot*, 3–5 New York: Random House.

INDEX

INDEX

INDEX